Praise f

"If you have ever struggl[...]
and loves you passionatel[...]
bring you comfort, hope and deep joy. Even if you have embraced that
truth for years, this book will take you deeper."

—Sheila Walsh, author of *God Loves Broken People*

"*Unexpected Love* is a breath of fresh air in a world of stuffy religious
ideas and disgruntled worshipers. It is impossible to read this book and
not get excited about the unconditional love of the Savior for women—
ALL women! This love letter in book form will draw readers into a closer
relationship with the very God of the universe."

—Kathi Macias, award-winning author of forty books,
including the 2011 Golden Scrolls Novel of the
Year and Carol Award Finalist, *Red Ink*. Visit her at
www.kathimacias.com or www.boldfiction.com.

"The love of Christ is so undeserved, so unexpected, yet He gives it
freely. Julie Coleman has woven this unexpected love into stories that
not only teach but lead us to expect what God promises fully—all His
love. Well written, spoken from the heart, *Unexpected Love* brings you
closer to the God who cares so much for you. This book has earned a
spot on my nightstand, an arm's reach to refreshment.

—Cindy Sproles, author and executive
editor of ChristianDevotions.us

"Every now and then one finds a new Christian author with a passion for
the Word of God which expresses itself though wondrous insights into
people and into Christ Himself, things that are fresh but ring totally
true. Julie Coleman is such an author. With a careful sense of both text
and context, Coleman unravels deep Scriptural mysteries with conviction and wit, using questions and answers to help modern women probe
to see how Jesus related to women then and discover how He ministers
to and through them now."

—Dr. Ken Quick, author of *Healing the Heart of Your
Church* and professor at Capital Bible Seminary

"Part storyteller, part teacher, and part trusted friend, Julie invites you to explore how Jesus met the women in his world with life-enriching, unexpected love. Join her, and you'll encounter a Savior who is just as crazy about you."

—LEIGH MCLEROY, SPEAKER AND AUTHOR OF *THE BEAUTIFUL ACHE, THE SACRED ORDINARY*, AND *TREASURED*

"Have you ever longed for significance, acceptance, or affection? *Unexpected Love* passionately speaks to the heart of every woman. In it Julie Coleman clearly communicates biblical accounts of Christ's value, compassion, and unconditional love for women, their need for a Savior, and His ultimate sacrifice to satisfy that need. This is the book you've been waiting for."

—TAMMY BENNETT, STRATEGIST, SBC OF VIRGINIA WOMEN'S MINISTRY, AND AUTHOR OF *101 MAKEOVER MINUTES: QUICK TIPS FOR LOOKING GOOD FROM THE INSIDE OUT*

"Julie Coleman is a fantastic storyteller! In her book, *Unexpected Love*, she pairs her gift for storytelling with solid Bible study to bring depth to Jesus' interactions with women. My heart was delighted. My perspective was challenged. My life with God was enriched by reading and applying this book."

—ÚNA F. LUCEY-LEE, REGIONAL LEADERSHIP DEVELOPMENT COORDINATOR, GREAT LAKES WEST REGION, INTERVARSITY CHRISTIAN FELLOWSHIP; CONTRIBUTING AUTHOR, *SMALL GROUP LEADERS' HANDBOOK: DEVELOPING TRANSFORMATIONAL COMMUNITIES* (IVP)

"Whether you've struggled to understand the difficult conversations that Jesus had with women or wrestled with comprehending the Lord's voice in your own life, you must read *Unexpected Love*. Julie Coleman, with incredible attention and scholarship, invites the reader on a journey into first-century Judea where a patriarchal society clashes with a God on a mission to rescue the hearts of all mankind, including women."

—JUSTIN HIBBARD, PASTOR OF NEW HOPE CHAPEL, ARNOLD, MARYLAND

"Julie's fresh insights into familiar stories of New Testament women who encountered Jesus will deepen your own relationship with Him. This is a book I will read again and again . . . and purchase for friends. I'm *not* giving my copy away!"

—MARLENE BAGNULL, WRITE HIS ANSWERS MINISTRIES, DIRECTOR OF THE COLORADO WRITERS CONFERENCE AND FOUNDER AND DIRECTOR OF THE GREATER PHILLY CHRISTIAN WRITERS CONFERENCE

"*Unexpected Love* is an unexpected delight! From extensive research and an inspired imagination, Julie Coleman brings to life New Testament stories of Jesus and the women with whom He interacted. Each chapter of *Unexpected Love* paints a captivating account, followed by probing questions, many of which I myself have wondered in the past. This fresh look at how Jesus related to the women of His day is both relevant and essential for us now. I heartily recommend Julie's book to women of all ages who want a richer relationship with their Savior."

—NANCY SEBASTIAN MEYER, AUTHOR OF *SPIRITUALLY SINGLE MOMS: RAISING GODLY KIDS WHEN DAD DOESN'T BELIEVE* (NAVPRESS) WWW.HOPE4HEARTS.NET

"Like the women recounted in the pages of this book, I am reminded that I like the person I am when I am with Jesus. And, I see anew how He longs to dream through me . . . and you . . . for His glory. What a message of hope, value, and purpose!"

—MARILYN N. ANDERES, NATIONAL SPEAKER AND AUTHOR OF *MORE*

"*Unexpected Love* is beautifully written, scholarly researched, sensitive to the Jewish milieu in which the events occurred, and wonderfully practical. If you are looking for a text that is useful for sermon preparation, Bible study groups, or personal benefit that is biblically sound, faithful to the Jewish world in which the events took place, and helpful for your own walk with the Lord, this is a book you need to have."

—GARY DERECHINSKY, MDIV, PASTOR AT BETH ARIEL MESSIANIC CONGREGATION, CANOGA PARK, CALIFORNIA

unexpected love

unexpected love

GOD'S HEART REVEALED IN JESUS'
CONVERSATIONS WITH WOMEN

BY JULIE ZINE COLEMAN

THOMAS NELSON
Since 1798

NASHVILLE   DALLAS   MEXICO CITY   RIO DE JANEIRO

Published in Nashville, Tennessee, by Thomas Nelson. Thomas Nelson is a registered trademark of Thomas Nelson, Inc.

Thomas Nelson, Inc., titles may be purchased in bulk for educational, business, fundraising, or sales promotional use. For information, please e-mail SpecialMarkets@ ThomasNelson.com.

Unless otherwise noted, Scripture quotations are taken from the New American Standard Bible®, © The Lockman Foundation 1960, 1962, 1963, 1968, 1971, 1972, 1973, 1975, 1977, 1995. Used by permission.

Scripture quotations marked NKJV are from The New King James Version®. © 1982 by Thomas Nelson, Inc. Used by permission. All rights reserved.

Scripture quotations marked NLT are from the *Holy Bible*, New Living Translation. © 1996, 2004, 2007. Used by permission of Tyndale House Publishers, Inc., Wheaton, Illinois 60189. All rights reserved.

Scripture quotations marked NIV are taken from the Holy Bible, New International Version®, NIV®. © 1973, 1978, 1984, 2011 by Biblica, Inc.™ Used by permission of Zondervan. All rights reserved worldwide. www.zondervan.com.

Scripture quotations marked NAB are from the Catholic Edition of the Revised Standard Version of the Bible. © 1965, 1966. National Council of the Churches of Christ in the United States of America. Used by permission. All rights reserved.

Library of Congress Cataloging-in-Publication Data

Coleman, Julie Zine, 1957-
  Unexpected love : God's heart revealed in Jesus' conversations with women / by Julie Zine Coleman.
    p. cm.
  Includes bibliographical references.
  ISBN 978-1-4002-0424-3
1. Women in the Bible. 2. Bible. N.T. Gospels--Biography. I. Title.
  BS2445.C65 2013
  226'.0922082--dc23

Printed in the United States of America

13 14 15 16 17 QG 6 5 4 3 2 1

For my husband, Steve
My partner in life, wise counselor,
spiritual leader, selfless servant, best friend

Contents

————

Contents

Introduction

———

$\mathscr{A}$s she leaned over to draw water from the well, she was startled to hear the stranger speak. "Give me a drink?" he asked. She almost dropped her jar.

Of course she had noticed him as she approached the well, sitting alone on the low stone wall surrounding the well's opening. Mostly she had noticed he was a Jew by the telltale band of blue around the hem of his garment. Jews were not known for their friendliness there in Samaria. They regarded her people as unclean, and most would never deign to speak with a Samaritan. Yet here he was, striking up a conversation. With a *female* Samaritan, no less!

She had to ask. "How is it that you, being Jewish and all, are asking me, a Samaritan woman, for a drink?"

He smiled kindly at her. "If you knew who was asking, *you* would be requesting what *I* could give you: living water."

Thus began the strange conversation that would change her life forever.

It was an unusual occurrence in first-century Israel for a

man to speak with any woman in public, especially a stranger. First-century rabbinic writings warned that women were prone to promiscuity and lechery.[1] For this reason, rabbis were forbidden to even greet a woman in public for fear of succumbing to her seduction.[2] Some Pharisees were actually called the "bruised and bleeding" because they shut their eyes to avoid even visual contact with a woman and subsequently walked into walls![3]

Attitudes at the time of Christ in the world at large were strongly influenced by the Greek Hellenistic culture established in the previous century. Considered vastly inferior to men, women were thought of as fickle, contentious, and indecisive.[4] They were given very few legal rights and lived under their fathers' control and then their husbands' for their lifetimes.[5]

In Israel, women received neither formal education nor instruction in the Torah. One rabbi wrote the Scripture should be burned rather than "entrusted to a woman."[6] In their daily prayers, men routinely gave a word of thanks that God had not made them a woman.[7]

If you were born female, life in this strictly patriarchal society was often an exercise in humility and subjugation.

God did not originally intend this for women. At the time of creation, he created Adam *and* Eve in his own image. When Adam first laid eyes on Eve, he observed, "This is now bone of my bones, and flesh of my flesh." At last! Someone like me— with whom to talk, exchange ideas, share dreams! Scripture remarks, "For this reason a man shall . . . be joined to his wife; and they shall become one flesh."[8]

It was an equal partnership, a complementary fitting

Introduction

established there in the garden of Eden. Each was created to fill the other's need for companionship and comfort. The idea of authority and domination would be instituted later—after the fall.

Everything changed with the first sin. Man, woman, and serpent all suffered grave consequences for their disobedience. One dramatic change came in the relationship between Adam and Eve. "Your desire will be for your husband," God told Eve, "and he will rule over you."[9] From that day forward women would spend millennia existing under the oppression of a male-dominated society. First-century Israel was no exception.

But Jesus came to set them free.

On the cross, Christ paid the ransom for humankind, setting us free from the condemnation and power of sin. But his redemption provided even more. We were also delivered from the consequences of sin. "You have been bought with a price," Paul reminded the Corinthians.[10] The original Greek word for that kind of purchase literally meant deliverance from the slave marketplace, provision of a new setting. With his purchase, Christ removed the Curse. He intended to restore women to the glory that they had at creation.

Nowhere can we see that intent better displayed than in Jesus' conversations with women.

At first glance, these gospel accounts inspire more questions than answers. While we applaud his interest in women and his willingness to publicly encounter them, we cringe at what could be construed as insensitive or callous behavior. How could Jesus respond to a woman desperately pleading for her child first by ignoring her, then calling her a dog? Why would he force the woman with an embarrassing medical condition to admit her ailment to the whole town? How could he speak so disrespectfully to his mother as she called his attention to a shortage of wine at a wedding celebration?

These encounters are easily misunderstood if we take them out of the cultural and literary contexts in which they occur. But when we view them in light of these contexts, a concerned, sensitive, and purposeful Jesus emerges. Most women approached him with a physical need or request. Jesus wanted to give them more than a temporary fix. He wanted to transform their lives.

So he started with where they were, with what they believed, with what they thought they needed. And as they conversed, he moved them forward, to a place where they could know him and ultimately understand what they truly needed. His desire was for a relationship with them. He wanted their hearts.

The women of the first century were not so different from women of today. They struggled with a need for significance, a need to be loved. They forged their way in this world, fulfilling their responsibilities and trying to make their lives count for something. In the end, nothing would fill them up, make them content, or give meaning to the day-to-day struggle to survive but a relationship with Jesus Christ.

It is what they needed most of all. So Christ set out to give it to them. And in finding that authentic relationship, one based on faith alone, each woman found true peace and meaning. Knowing Christ made all the difference.

So join me in taking a closer look at each of these encounters. We will find more than miracles performed or simple conversations. What we will discover in these narratives is

Jesus' heart for those he met. What you will read will enrich your relationship with him.

He was crazy about women.

He is crazy about you.

chapter one

On the third day there was a wedding in Cana of Galilee, and the mother of Jesus was there; and both Jesus and His disciples were invited to the wedding. When the wine ran out, the mother of Jesus said to Him, "They have no wine."

And Jesus said to her, "Woman, what does that have to do with us? My hour has not yet come."

His mother said to the servants, "Whatever He says to you, do it."

Now there were six stone waterpots set there for the Jewish custom of purification, containing twenty or thirty gallons each. Jesus said to them, "Fill the waterpots with water." So they filled them up to the brim. And He said to them, "Draw some out now and take it to the headwaiter." So they took it to him.

When the headwaiter tasted the water which had become wine, and did not know where it came from (but the servants who had drawn the water knew), the headwaiter called the bridegroom, and said to him, "Every man serves the good wine first, and when the people have drunk freely, then he serves the poorer wine; but you have kept the good wine until now."

This beginning of His signs Jesus did in Cana of Galilee, and manifested His glory, and His disciples believed in Him.

—JOHN 2:1–11

Mother Doesn't Always Know Best

JESUS AND MARY AT THE WEDDING AT CANA

It is an embarrassing situation. The host has run out of wine, and the party is still going strong. Mary brings the problem to her son Jesus, who does not respond as she thought he would. Their resulting interchange is disconcerting to the reader. What is she really asking him to do? Is he being disrespectful to his mother in his response? What was the significance of making this his first miracle?

The wedding began as so many others through the years in Cana. A noisy, joyful group left the groom's house and paraded through the streets, accompanying him on his mission to collect his bride. Music announced the boisterous procession as they wound their way, finally arriving at the bride's home.

3

Both bride and groom were crowned in garlands and led back to the groom's home. Friends and family carried lamps and torches to light the way. People from the town lined the route to cheer on the procession and, once it had passed them, joined in.

Upon the group's arrival at the groom's home, a formal, legal agreement was signed, and the groom promised to care for his new wife, keeping her in the manner of the men of Israel.[1] The couple was led to the marriage bed and left in privacy to consummate the union. The marriage ceremony was now complete, and the party began in earnest.

Guests filled the house to enjoy the abundant food and wine. Happiness and goodwill flooded the residence as friends and family celebrated the joyous occasion. They would remain for a week or more, eating, drinking, and socializing. The groom's parents considered their hospitality an act of religious significance, following the example of Abraham and David. It was important to all Jews that they welcome their guests and aptly provide for their comfort and needs.[2]

At one point, Mary, who was helping with the festivities, looked up from a conversation to see a worried servant approaching. He quietly informed her of a problem: they had run out of wine. Mary winced. The celebration showed no signs of slowing down. To fail to provide for their guests' needs would prove humiliating for the hosts, to say the least.

After racking her brain for a minute or two, Mary turned to seek her son, whom she knew might furnish a solution. Moving her gaze around the room, she spotted him close to the entryway, laughing with a few of the other guests and his newly avowed disciples. Mary hurried to where they stood and pulled him aside. Jesus and his five disciples moved with her into the entryway.

"Jesus, they are out of wine," she informed him. Jesus' eyes met Mary's. Both of them knew the implications of the unforeseen shortage on the groom's family. The disciples looked at each other. What did she expect Jesus to do? They had just arrived in town, with little money between them and no connections with the people of Cana.

Jesus answered her, "Woman, what does that have to do with me? My hour has not yet come."

Mary steadily returned his gaze. She felt confident that Jesus would somehow find the right thing to do. He had taken care of things for his family since his father's passing. She trusted him to manage this as well.

Mary turned to the servants who followed her, still anxiously awaiting her direction. "Do whatever he says to you," she simply instructed them.

Jesus pointed to the six large stone waterpots standing nearby on the floor. Much of the water they originally contained was long gone, used for traditional cleansing rites performed by host and guests in the preceding days. "Fill these waterpots back up to the brim," he instructed. The disciples watched the servants move quickly to do his bidding, wondering as they fulfilled their task. How would more water solve the problem?

Once finished, the servants stood back, waiting for the next instruction. Jesus surprised them by saying, "Draw some out now and take it to the headwaiter." Why would the headwaiter want to taste the water? And what about the wine? Why wasn't Jesus doing something about that?

One servant moved forward, lifted the ladle, and began to pour the water into a goblet. To his shock and to the astonishment of those watching, what poured from the ladle looked like rich red wine! What in the world? Hadn't they just filled the pots with water?

Hands shaking, the servant took the goblet to the headwaiter. The man, who had no clue that anything unusual was afoot, took a healthy gulp. A look of appreciation came over his face. Obviously this was a new batch of wine being introduced. The quality difference was unmistakable. How unusual to serve the superior wine in the latter part of the celebration!

The disciples watched in amazement as the headwaiter called across the room to the bridegroom. "I just tasted the new wine," he told him. "Usually at occasions like this, the host brings out the finest wine at the beginning, when people are thirsty and will most appreciate quality fare. Once people have drunk freely, they lose their discerning palate and don't notice the inferior wine served later on in the celebration. But you, sir, have saved the best for last!"

The guests cheered and held up their goblets to be filled again. Servants quickly ladled the wine into pitchers and began liberally distributing it among the crowd. With such an abundance, running out was no longer a concern. The celebration, rejuvenated by the introduction of fine wine, continued into the night.

Mary stood at the door of the room, smiling, enjoying the pleasure of the guests. The disciples huddled together, discussing what they had just witnessed. During the past few days, Jesus had impressed them with his powerful words and inexplicable insight. Today he revealed a different kind of power, defying the natural world and proving he was no ordinary man. Seeing this incredible miracle sealed the deal for them. They now firmly believed he was the Messiah.

Digging Deeper

What did Mary know about Jesus as Messiah?

How much did Mary understand about her son in his formative years? From the beginning, it was certainly obvious that he was no ordinary child. An angel announced to her that he would be conceived by the Holy Spirit, not by normal human means. He would be great, would rule on the throne of his ancestor David, and would be called the "Son of God."[3] Joseph was told to name him Jesus, "for he will save His people from their sins."[4]

Her older cousin Elizabeth, mother of John the Baptist, was moved by the Holy Spirit to call Mary "the mother of my Lord."[5] The night of Jesus' birth, he was visited by shepherds, who shared the angels' announcement that sent them to the stable: "For today in the city of David there has been born for you a Savior, who is Christ the Lord."[6] (The name *Christ* is Greek for "anointed one" and was a commonly used title for the promised deliverer of Israel.)

When he was eight days old, his parents took him to the temple in nearby Jerusalem to be dedicated and presented to the Lord. There the baby was prophesied over by Simeon and Anna, who both confirmed him to be the salvation of Israel.[7] Sometime later they received a visit from unusually distinguished guests: wise men from the East came bearing gifts and worshipped the little boy.[8]

While we know what Mary saw and heard in the days surrounding his birth, we don't know how much she really understood. We are only told she "treasured all these things, pondering them in her heart."[9]

Not long after his birth, Jesus' parents were warned in a dream to leave Bethlehem and go to Egypt for a time.[10] They narrowly escaped Herod's attempt to remove a perceived threat to his throne: he murdered all of Bethlehem's little boys aged two and under. Once Herod died and the coast was clear, Joseph and Mary were directed by another dream to return to Galilee, back to their hometown of Nazareth, with their little son.[11] There they settled down and made a life for their new family.

Mary's husband, Joseph, was a carpenter by trade. He and Mary raised their family in the isolated, insignificant village on the limited income of a hand laborer. It was an inauspicious beginning for a king.

The only other information we have about Jesus' formative years is an account given by Luke of a family trip to Jerusalem when he was twelve. They had gone to celebrate the Passover, traveling with a caravan of relatives and friends from home. On the way back, Joseph and Mary, assuming he was with friends, eventually discovered that Jesus was missing, probably when they made camp for the evening and gathered the family together to eat. Sick with worry, the couple hurried back to the city and searched for three harrowing days. Finally they found him sitting calmly in the temple dialoguing with teachers of the Law. Mary, emotional from three days of anxiety, sobbed out her angst and relief: "Son, why have you treated us like this? Here your father and I have been anxiously searching for you!"

Jesus looked up, sincerely surprised that his parents would have worried. "Why were you searching for me?" he asked them. "Didn't you know that I must be involved in my Father's interests?"

Luke summed up the parent-child relationship for the remaining pre-adult years with these simple words: "He went down with them and came to Nazareth, and He continued in subjection to them."[12]

First-century Jewish culture gave a mother full control over her sons until they reached the age of thirteen. She was fully responsible to train them in obedience, character, and morality according to the law of Moses. Once a boy reached the age of thirteen, the father took over, apprenticing his son in a trade and taking him to the synagogue for spiritual instruction.[13] Because Joseph probably died sometime between Jesus' age of twelve and thirty, Mary may have been involved with Jesus' later upbringing more directly than most mothers.[14]

In many aspects it is hard to imagine being the mother of the Son of God. By the time he was thirty, Jesus fully understood who he was and what he had come to do. But how much did he understand when he was, say, five years old? What would the many mother-son conversations over the years have contained? What did she need to teach him? Luke's words seem to infer a definite learning curve as Jesus grew up: "Jesus kept increasing in wisdom and stature, and in favor with God and men."[15] Surely Mary must have recounted the many things God revealed around the time of his birth. Did he, in turn, share his growing knowledge with her as it was revealed to him? We'll never know. But certainly she must have felt especially purposeful as she endeavored to raise this special child.

Why would Mary go to Jesus to solve the wine problem when he had never performed a miracle before?

Mary knew, of course, Jesus was the Messiah. It is possible she heard about the events in the days immediately preceding the wedding—maybe from his disciples. He'd gone into the wilderness to be baptized by John the Baptist, and as he came up out of the water, God's spirit descended from the sky like a dove. A voice from heaven declared: "You are My beloved Son, in You I am well-pleased."[16] Jesus then spent forty days in the wilderness in prayer and mental preparation for what lay ahead. When he returned, he began taking on disciples, telling them, "You will see the heavens opened and the angels of God ascending and descending on the Son of Man."[17]

Things had begun to happen. Was this the beginning of a new phase for her son? If Mary was aware of these things, she may have thought the situation was the perfect opportunity for him to make public his identity. What better way to announce he was the Messiah than by miraculously solving their host's problem for a ready-made crowd? No doubt (as any proud mother would) she had lived the past thirty years in eager anticipation for the time his true identity would finally be revealed.

So Mary approached Jesus, presenting him with what she saw as a golden opportunity. Maybe God himself had orchestrated these circumstances for that very purpose! Jesus' response shows he didn't see it that way: "Woman, what does that have to do with us? My hour has not yet come."

Was Jesus being disrespectful of Mary in the way he spoke to her?

Jesus' words to Mary have been interpreted with widely differing views. We must look at his reply from a historical-cultural perspective as well as within the context of the biblical text to correctly hear what he said.

First, Jesus called his mother *woman*. I'm pretty sure that my mother would not have appreciated my using such a title in talking to her. But then again, we are centuries removed from the original cultural context. *Woman* was neither an unusual nor an offensive term of address. We find two examples in other ancient literature. In Homer's *Iliad*, the Greek hero Odysseus addresses his beloved wife as *woman*. Within that same general time period, Augustus Caesar used the same title for the revered Egyptian queen Cleopatra.[18] In both cases, *woman* was used with respect and fondness.

Later in John, Jesus called his mother *woman* once again. This time it was from the cross, as he hung near death's door. "Woman," he gasped, indicating the disciple John standing by her side. "Behold, your son!" Then he looked at John and instructed, "Behold, your mother!" compelling him to care for Mary in the difficult days ahead.[19] The situation certainly indicates a tone of tenderness and concern. Clearly the address was not intended to be insulting in the least.

After calling her *woman*, Jesus asked his mother a puzzling question. The New American Standard Bible translates it, "What does that have to do with us?" The phrase is actually a Greek idiom, which is literally translated, "What to me and to you?" Demons used the same idiom when Jesus confronted them, and it is translated, "What business do we have with each other, Jesus, Son of the Most High God?"[20]

Many commentators suggest Jesus was drawing a line in the sand. Mary had overstepped her bounds. She was trying to assert her parental authority over him, failing to understand her son's mission. His response was a rebuke, an intentional disengagement, meant to distance himself from her.

The problem with this interpretation is its inconsistency with the way that the rest of Scripture depicts the character of Christ. Would Jesus treat his mother with such callous disregard, especially in light of the concern she had just expressed for the wedding hosts? Jesus was well aware of the fifth commandment: honor your father and mother.[21] He would later rebuke the Pharisees for neglecting this very command because of ministry priorities.[22] It is inconsistent to think that Jesus would turn his back on his mother for the sake of ministry when he pointed out this practice as erroneous in others.

So what did Jesus intend to say with this puzzling phrase?

It is helpful to compare this conversation with a second conversation sharing an identical structure: Jesus' interaction with the Syrophoenician woman (covered fully in chapter 4). She also came to Jesus with a request: that he would deliver her daughter from demon possession. Jesus did not positively respond to her expressed need either—in fact, he also refused her at first. Then he gave a reason why he should not help, just as he did at Cana.

What turned the tide in both conversations? Expressions of faith. Jesus commended the Syrophoenician woman for her faith. He then granted her request.

By instructing the servants to do as Jesus asked, Mary was expressing faith in Jesus. She was content to let Jesus work things out in his own way, in his own time. As with the Syrophoenician woman, Jesus responded to her faith with a miracle.

His initial refusal in both accounts is really a means to an end. He is driving them further in their trust relationship with him. His puzzling words are merely a way to move them forward.

What was "the hour" to which Jesus referred?

"My hour has not yet come," Jesus explained to his mother. To what hour was Jesus referring?

We can certainly eliminate a couple of possibilities of what Jesus meant by observing his ensuing actions. As soon as he finished speaking with Mary, he went ahead and performed the miracle. So obviously Jesus was not telling her it was not the time he would start doing miracles. Nor could it have been an expression of unwillingness to help their hapless hosts, because he did go ahead and solve their problem.

So what *was* Jesus talking about?

In the book of John, he used similar language when his brothers urged him to go up to Jerusalem and make his messiahship public. "No one does anything in secret when he himself seeks to be known publicly. If You do these things, show Yourself to the world," they told him. Jesus responded to their advice: "Go up to the feast yourselves; I do not go up to this feast because *My time has not yet fully come*."[23]

Jesus then went on to do exactly what he said he wouldn't.

He made the trip to Jerusalem, just as they suggested. But John was careful to point out that Jesus' reason for being in Jerusalem was opposite from what his brothers suggested: "He Himself also went up, *not publicly, but as if, in secret.*"[24] Going to Jerusalem was not the problem. It was plans to make a public announcement there that concerned him.

John also cited two instances when people wanted to seize him but were unable to accomplish that because "His hour had not yet come."[25]

Later in John's book Jesus indicated what would happen when the hour arrived. "The hour has come for the Son of Man to be glorified," he told his disciples. "Unless a grain of wheat falls into the earth and dies, it remains alone; but if it dies, it bears much fruit . . . My soul has become troubled; and what shall I say, 'Father, save Me from this hour'? But for this purpose I came to this hour."[26]

The hour to which Jesus referred was the time when he would be crucified, buried, and resurrected. Only after this series of events had occurred would his identity be revealed openly.

Why was Jesus unwilling to make a big public announcement at the beginning of his ministry?

The Jews had waited many centuries for the Messiah to appear. His coming had been foretold from the time of the first sin, when God handed down the consequences of disobedience in the garden of Eden. The promise of the Messiah's coming was reiterated to Abraham, Jacob, Moses, and David. The prophets spoke of the great kingdom and reign he would inaugurate at his coming. The Messiah was the hope of Israel, and the people greatly anticipated the blessing and restoration his reign would bring.

But the people overlooked an important part of the prophets' message. There were two distinct pictures of the Messiah, portrayed side by side in Old Testament prophecy. One was of a messiah who would come in power and rule the earth. The other was of a suffering servant. In hindsight, we now know that these were two sides of the same Messiah, descriptions of his two separate comings. The first time he appeared, he would suffer and die for the sin of the world. At his return he would come and take his rightful place on the throne.

The people did not understand this. They only anticipated the powerful king who would lead them to overthrow the Romans and establish autonomy again. If word got around that the Messiah had arrived, the masses would have rallied to revolt. There was already a sizable group known as the Zealots, readying themselves to do just that. But Jesus had not come to overthrow an earthly government. He had come to offer not political but spiritual freedom, releasing his people from the power of sin, and he would accomplish this on the cross. Before that climactic event, however, there was preliminary work to be done. He needed to teach about his kingdom and validate his words with miracles. He needed to train disciples to carry on the building of his kingdom once he was gone.

So for the time being, Jesus needed to keep his identity under wraps. There would be no big announcement until after the hour of his death and resurrection. The time for that was still several years away.

Why was this the first miracle? Was there some significance in turning water into wine?

As we read through the first several chapters of John's gospel, a theme begins to emerge. Much of what he relates has something to do with water.

The first event portrayed is Jesus' baptism in the waters of the Jordan River. Soon afterward, John the Baptist testified, "I came baptizing in water . . . but He . . . baptizes in the Holy Spirit."[27] Physical water alone would not remove sin. Jesus' ministry would be spiritual in nature, doing what physical water could never do: provide eternal life.

In chapter 4, Jesus had a conversation with a Samaritan woman who came to draw water at the well. The entire conversation revolved around his offer of living water. He told her, "Whoever drinks of the water that I will give him shall never thirst; but . . . [it] will become in him a well of water springing up to eternal life."[28] Once again, we see a contrast of physical water to the spiritual work of Christ.

One more account, seen in chapter 5, completes the picture John was drawing for us. A man who had been ill for thirty-eight years awaited his turn to enter the waters of the pool of Bethesda, thought to give physical healing on occasion. Jesus approached him and with a word healed the man of his physical ailment, telling him to pick up his pallet and walk. (Later, Jesus sought him out in the temple and addressed his spiritual need as well.) The Pharisees who witnessed the miraculous incident could only criticize the man for carrying his pallet on the Sabbath. Their eyes were clearly focused on the physical here and now, while Christ's agenda went far beyond that into the spiritual realm.

The wedding at Cana is nestled within the context of these comparisons repeatedly being made between physical water (representing the earthly and temporary) and the work of Jesus (spiritual and eternal in nature).

There is another interesting detail. John was careful to mention that the water involved in the Cana miracle was the water used for Jewish purification rites. A devoutly Jewish wedding ceremony would have needed a substantial amount of water for the many ceremonial cleansings. As the guests arrived, their feet were washed to remove the dirt from the road. Then before each meal, and between each course, hands were carefully washed to keep the people from ceremonial uncleanliness.[29] Each of these rituals was not to maintain hygiene but to remove religious impurity.[30] They were regulations developed by the predecessors of the Pharisees, whose idea of holiness had been reduced to keeping a set of arbitrary rules. For them it was no longer about a relationship with God. It was simply a religion.

The six twenty- to thirty-gallon jars stood in the entryway, their contents purposed for legalistic pharisaical standards. It was no coincidence Jesus chose this particular water to transform into wine.

Jesus had come to offer something far superior to the pharisaical way. People could never earn their way into God's favor by keeping the Law, for they would inevitably fail. Another way had to be provided. God's plan was for his Son to make atonement for the sin of the world by taking the punishment for the guilty as a substitutionary sacrifice. By simply believing in him, one could enter into an eternal relationship with God. Salvation would come through grace.

Jesus had come to usher in a huge change, a way vastly superior to the Pharisees' religion. It would be like, well, comparing water to wine.

The salvation Jesus would offer was not a supplement to the pharisaical way. It was a replacement. The two are poles apart. Jesus described the incompatibility with another wine allegory: "No one puts new wine into old wineskins; otherwise the wine will burst the skins, and the wine is lost and the skins as well; but one puts new wine into fresh wineskins."[31] Trying to make the old align with the new was just not possible.

Beginning his ministry with this particular miracle was strategically brilliant. It defined his intentions toward the religious ideas currently in place, defying the pharisaical concept of holiness. It set the tone for what was to follow, symbolizing what his coming would bring. Something fresh. New. Better.

Wine was also one of the symbols in Old Testament prophecy that pictured the presence of the Messiah. The prophet Amos offered this description of his kingdom: "The mountains will drip sweet wine and all the hills will be dissolved."[32] Jesus' turning water into wine as the first miracle sent an unmistakable, albeit subtle, message: the Promised One had arrived.

For Today's Woman

We can take a cue from Mary's example the day of the wedding celebration. What she knew about Jesus ultimately determined what she said and what she did.

God had revealed a lot of information to Mary, especially

in the time period surrounding the birth of her son. Much of it was difficult to comprehend. Yet even when a complete understanding was beyond her, she chose to trust in the wisdom and goodness of God. She submitted herself to his instructions and made herself available to be used by him. Her trusting response to Jesus at the wedding echoed the submissive response she had at the announcement of his conception: "Behold, the bondslave of the Lord; may it be done to me according to your word."[33]

Mary might not have completely understood each revelation given to her, but the faith she exercised was not blind faith. It was based on what she knew to be true about God. Her knowledge was based on scriptures that were very familiar to her. We find evidence of this in her spontaneous burst of praise known as the Magnificat. In it she quoted from Habakkuk, Isaiah, the Psalms, 1 Samuel, Genesis, and Malachi.[34] She also referred to promises made to Abraham and their fulfillment, God's power displayed in his mighty deeds, and his mercy given to generations. Mary knew much about God.

The first step to trusting God as Mary did is in getting to know him. But be careful where you get your information. It needs to be consistent with what he reveals about himself in his Word.

On the first day of second grade, a teacher friend of mine showed her students the birthday bulletin board. She remarked that one child had a "special birthday." When he asked why his was special, Shelly explained that she and the student shared that birthday. They were born on the same day!

The little second grader slowly looked his middle-aged teacher up and down. "I don't think so," he replied, shaking his head.

Like that little guy, we may have a faulty assumption that will lead us to a faulty conclusion. We all have ideas about who God is and what he is like. We base our expectations of how he will act on those ideas. Then when God acts in unexpected ways, we become disillusioned with him. But God did not let us down. Only our faulty, preconceived ideas of God disappointed us.

God has revealed all we need to know about him in his Word. We need to make it our business to find out what that is. When we know of his power, his goodness, his wisdom, his patience, and his justice, we have a reason to put our trust in him. And we will not be disappointed when our trust is based on truth.

The better we know him, the greater our ability will be to trust him even when he does the unexpected.

Mary had ideas on how Jesus' ministry would unfold. She spent thirty years in anticipation of the time her son the Messiah would be revealed. It sure seemed like the time had come. Jesus had already begun moving forward, leaving town, getting baptized, and gathering disciples. When the wine ran out at a largely attended gathering, Mary must have thought this was *it*. Jesus would supply the need of his hosts and reveal his identity in one fell swoop. The situation seemed a godsend.

Then Jesus told her differently. He would be revealed to the world as the Messiah, but only later on, when he had accomplished the work he had come to do. The hour of his glorification had not come. Mary understood *what* he meant, but it is doubtful she understood *why*. Jesus didn't explain. Mary took him at his word. She knew God's ways and timing are always best. So she chose to trust even when she didn't understand.

When I graduated from college back in 1979, finding employment as an elementary school teacher was a grim prospect. Every advertised position received a flood of hundreds of applications. I was not dissuaded. I knew with every fiber of my being that God wanted me to teach. So I waited expectantly for his provision of a job near my hometown in Connecticut. It was a long summer.

My big break finally came several weeks after the school year started. A Christian school in Maryland had just lost a first grade teacher due to a serious illness. Was I still available?

Maryland? To a homegrown New Englander, that seemed like the other side of the world. But a job was a job. As I packed my bags to head south, my mother sat on my bed, fretting. "I'm so afraid you will end up staying there forever," she told me.

I laughed at her fears. "Don't worry, Mom," I assured her. "If there is one thing that I can tell you for sure, it is this: I'll be back. I will *not* live in Maryland for the rest of my life." Several weeks after settling into my new job, I met the man who became my husband. The rest is history: we have lived in Maryland for all but two of our thirty-two years together. I had my plans. God had other, superior plans for me. I'm so glad we went with his. They may not have been what I expected, but I have been blessed beyond measure.

God frequently does the unexpected. Often, we don't ever learn the whys. Job never did. After all of the losses he endured, he was never told about the heavenly contest between God and Satan. God never revealed to him that he had been God's star example, that his faithfulness had proved to Satan that God could be worshipped for who he was, not just for what he provided. For thirty-seven chapters, Job cried out to

God, begging for comfort and answers. For thirty-seven chapters, Job got nothing. Then God finally spoke. But his was no warm, conciliatory answer. God basically told Job, "I'm God. That's all you need to know."

Job got it. He regretted he ever even thought to question God:

> *I know that You can do all things,*
> *And that no purpose of Yours can be thwarted. . . .*
> *Therefore I have declared that which I did not understand,*
> *Things too wonderful for me, which I did not know. . . .*
> *Now my eye sees You;*
> *Therefore I retract,*
> *And I repent in dust and ashes.*[35]

After seeing God revealed, it is a no-brainer to trust without question.

It is pretty much what Jesus told Mary. Yes, his identity would someday be revealed. But it would be in God's way, in God's timing. Mary knew Jesus and knew his commitment to obedience to his Father. It was all she needed to know in order to respond with trust.

There will be times in our lives when God asks the same of us. If Mary struggled with understanding, we should not be surprised when we do as well. God will act in unexpected and seemingly inexplicable ways. Sometimes the way will be filled with pain, causing suffering or terrible loss.

What should be our response? Knowing the perfect character of our God should guide our thoughts and actions. God is good all the time. There are things afoot that we may know nothing about. He is at work to bring glory to his name. He chooses to use us to achieve that purpose. We can trust in his wisdom.

Jesus accomplished several things with his first miracle. He proved his messiahship to his new disciples. He showed the character of his ministry, how it was a reversal of the current religious system touted by the Pharisees. But it did something for us as well. It shows us that no problem is too small to bring before the throne.

Just as he was concerned about the embarrassment of the hapless wedding hosts, God is concerned about the details of our lives. He is aware of every thought before we think it. He knows the number of hairs on our heads and tracks our every move.[36] He delights in his children.

Although he may work in mysterious ways, he does not send us to fend for ourselves on the journey. He does not miss one tear we cry.[37] His presence is a constant, even when we can't sense he is there. He carries us through the painful times and guides us through our uncertainty. We will emerge in the end, understanding him on a whole new level. In the end, his name will not be the only thing glorified. It will be worth it all.

৯ Food for Thought ৯

1. Paul wrote in 2 Timothy 1:12: "I know whom I have believed and I am convinced that He is able to guard what I have entrusted to Him until that day." Notice the progression that Paul expressed: first a knowledge of God, then trust. What part does your

knowledge of God play in your ability to trust him? What are ways you can move forward to be able to trust him even more?

2. Jesus always responded positively to faith. See Matthew 8:5–13. This man was a Gentile. What do Jesus' remarks to the man tell you about what he looked for in those around him?

3. How much faith is needed? See Mark 9:15–27. How much faith did the father have? Note his feeble declaration. How did Jesus respond? What does this tell you about Jesus' expectations?

4. God has a history of responding positively to faith. He also reacts strongly when it is refused him. Read Numbers 13:25–14:35. How did a lack of trust prompt God to act? What does this tell you about the importance he assigns to our trusting him?

✒ *Journaling* ✒

We are told that after receiving revelations from God, Mary "pondered them in her heart." Make it a point to write down your questions about God's working in your life. Under them, list what you know to be true about him that may apply to the circumstances.

Recording your thoughts is a way of storing them in your heart (as Mary did) until the day when God provides further insight.

He may never reveal the whys to you. Don't dwell on the circumstances. Rather, ponder the circumstance Maker. Let your questions lead you into a deeper understanding of who he is.

chapter two

When Jesus had crossed over again in the boat to the other side, a large crowd gathered around Him; and so He stayed by the seashore. One of the synagogue officials named Jairus came up, and on seeing Him, fell at His feet and implored Him earnestly, saying, "My little daughter is at the point of death; please come and lay Your hands on her, so that she will get well and live." And He went off with him; and a large crowd was following Him and pressing in on Him.

A woman who had had a hemorrhage for twelve years, and had endured much at the hands of many physicians, and had spent all that she had and was not helped at all, but rather had grown worse—after hearing about Jesus, she came up in the crowd behind Him and touched His cloak. For she thought, "If I just touch His garments, I will get well." Immediately the flow of her blood was dried up; and she felt in her body that she was healed of her affliction.

Immediately Jesus, perceiving in Himself that the power proceeding from Him had gone forth, turned around in the crowd and said, "Who touched My garments?"

And His disciples said to Him, "You see the crowd pressing in on You, and You say, 'Who touched Me?'" And He looked around to see the woman who had done this.

But the woman fearing and trembling, aware of what had happened to her, came and fell down before Him and told Him the whole truth.

And He said to her, "Daughter, your faith has made you well; go in peace and be healed of your affliction."

—MARK 5:21–34

(THIS STORY IS ALSO FOUND IN MATTHEW
9:18–26 AND LUKE 8:40–48.)

Embarrassed or Expunged?

JESUS AND THE HEMORRHAGING WOMAN

Desperate to find a cure for her condition, a woman approaches Jesus. She is not disappointed: one touch of his garment and she is instantly healed. While she would have happily returned home at that moment, grateful to be well, Jesus had more in mind for her. Why did he make her publicly admit her embarrassing condition? What significance does the pairing of her story and Jairus's daughter have to the meaning of this encounter?

She was so, so tired. Twelve years of bleeding and the resulting anemia had left her weak and barely able to function. Her search for a cure had resulted in nothing but disappointment. Doctor after doctor attempted to staunch the life-ebbing flow. She was sick to death of their ineffective potions and cures. Their bumbling, clumsy attentions had only seemed to make matters worse. Yet while their ministrations were ineffective, they had not been ashamed to charge their exorbitant fees. She was out of resources and out of hope.

Until this morning. Word had spread quickly through the town that the man who had healed people with leprosy and people unable to walk, and even unbelievably raised a young man from the dead, was returning to town. Jesus was coming! With desperate hope once again cautiously blooming in her heart, the woman joined the many by the docks awaiting his arrival. The crowd may have prevented her from seeing his boat, but she knew he had arrived by the sound of the crowd.

Voices called out as Jesus approached. Heart thumping, she waited silently for a chance to ask for his help. The crowd pressed in, desperate for a chance just to be near him. The sound of pleading voices swelled as the Master neared. Maybe if she could just touch a piece of his clothing. If she could just get close enough . . .

At that moment, the crowd parted as Jairus, a well-known synagogue official, pushed his way through to Jesus. He fell at his feet with a desperate request of his own. His beautiful, precious daughter was dying. She was only twelve years old. Wouldn't Jesus come to his house and heal her before it was too late?

The woman's breath caught in her throat. For as long as she had been bleeding, this little girl had been alive. Twelve years. The entire time she had slowly felt the life flow from her body, this little girl had been thriving and growing under the loving hand of this dedicated father. Now both the thriving and the waning were in the same desperate need of healing.

Jesus agreed to follow Jairus to his house. He began to walk again, moving right past where she stood. Knowing her window of opportunity was quickly closing, she pressed herself into the throng that surrounded the Master. Thrusting her arm out, she managed to touch one of the four corner fringes of his square prayer shawl resting on his shoulders.

In that moment, the unbelievable happened. Power surged through her body. Strength she hadn't known in twelve years suddenly filled her. The flow of blood, a dozen years long, just stopped cold. She was cured! As the crowd continued past her, she stood frozen in shock at what had just happened. Were her pain and suffering really over? After twelve long, painful years, had the affliction that had ostracized her from family and friends simply ceased to be?

Suddenly Jesus stopped. He turned and faced the crowd. "Who is the one who touched me?" he asked.

The disciples were amazed that he would ask such a question. He was surrounded by a host of people pressing up against him. How could he ask who touched him? A better question to ask was who didn't touch him!

Yet Jesus stood still, scanning the crowd. Heart in her throat, wishing she could sink into the ground, the woman remained rooted in her spot. She watched his eyes move over the people until they came to rest on her. And stopped. She began to tremble. Was he angry that she had just contaminated him with her touch? Expecting her to publicly confess what she had just done? As his eyes held hers, she felt compelled forward. Step by step, she approached him. She, like Jairus, fell at his feet.

How could she explain herself? Humiliated, she lifted her eyes to Jesus. But rather than be subjected to the condemnation she expected, she was surprised to see kindness in his eyes.

Haltingly she spoke through lips that would hardly work for her trembling. She explained as delicately as she could about her hemorrhaging. How her fingers had brushed the fringe. How she had been cured.

Jesus smiled into her eyes. She wanted to remain anonymous, just another woman in the crowd. Jesus wanted to make it personal. "Daughter," he gently said, "your faith has made you well." *Daughter!* Of all the ways to address her, this was the least expected. After twelve years of being an outcast, unclean, contaminating everything and everyone with the slightest touch, Jesus was calling her *daughter*?

Jesus continued. "Go in peace," he told her. "And be healed of your affliction."

Digging Deeper

What was the woman's problem?

Mark and Luke identify it as a flowing issue of blood (Greek, *rhysis haima*). Matthew calls it a hemorrhage (Greek, *haimorroeō*). In the Septuagint (an ancient Greek translation of the Old Testament), this word is used when referring to menstrual blood flow.[1] The woman had suffered virtually continuous menstrual bleeding for twelve years. The condition is known today as *menorrhagia*.

The ailment would have had several devastating impacts on her life. First were the physical effects of a constant blood loss. Anemia, an insufficient amount of red blood cells in the bloodstream, would have resulted. Red blood cells carry essential nutrients to all parts of the body. A deficient amount of red cells would mean an insufficient amount of oxygen and iron would be delivered to her vital organs. Her physical symptoms would have included muscle cramping, dizziness, fainting, and fatigue. Any physical exertion may have resulted in shortness of breath, rapid heartbeat, or even chest pain. The ailment would have affected her appearance as well: her complexion would have been wan and colorless.

My friend suffered from the same ailment some years ago. She was exhausted all of the time, barely functioning in her job as a teacher. At the end of the school day, she went home to family and church responsibilities: her husband was a pastor of a large congregation. Hers was one full plate, and until her hysterectomy the condition kept her from fulfilling the most basic tasks. "I can't even write on the blackboard anymore," she told me. "My arms ache terribly from the effort of just lifting the chalk up to write." For the hemorrhaging woman, living with anemia for twelve years must have been physically debilitating.

Second, the illness had left the woman financially destitute. She spent every resource on doctors in hopes of finding a cure. Unfortunately they offered nothing more than superstitious remedies, ineffectual at best, potentially harmful at worst. Eleven such "cures" used in those days are recorded in the Talmud.[2] One prescription was to carry around the ashes of an ostrich egg wrapped in a rag. Another was to carry a barley-corn husk, which had been found in the excrement of a white female donkey. An orally administered concoction consisted of wine combined with a compound made with rubber, alum, and a crocus bulb. Some even tried to scare away the infirmity, much like we would try to startle someone to stop hiccupping! With their exotic ingredients, the cost of these "cures" was extravagant. Twelve years of expensive and in-effectual treatments would have taken their toll.

A third impact of her ailment was perhaps the most dif-ficult to bear. According to Mosaic law, women with her disorder were to be considered unclean as long as they suffered from it. Leviticus 15:25–26 instructs: "Now if a woman has a discharge of her blood many days, not at the period of her menstrual impurity . . . she is unclean. Any bed on which she lies all the days of her discharge . . . and every thing on which she sits shall be unclean."

Earlier in Leviticus, the people were warned: "If [someone] touches human uncleanness . . . he will be guilty."[3] Anyone contaminated by contact with the woman would have had to undergo the inconvenience of a ritual cleansing process to rectify the contamination.[4] Therefore it is likely this woman's uncleanliness would have been known in the community; and those who knew about it likely would have avoided her. If she was married, sexual relations would have been permissible no longer, for they would have made her husband ceremonially unclean. Her condition might even have served as grounds for him to divorce her.[5]

So the woman had lived twelve long years in lonely isola-tion. No hugs, no warmth of touch could be received by or given to family or friends. She also was banned from the syna-gogue in her state of uncleanliness.[6] Hers had become a sad life of rejection, seemingly by God and man alike.

In short, the problem had ruined her life. It had impacted her health, her financial well-being, and her relationships. It's no wonder she determined to touch Jesus in the crowd, even knowing she would contaminate him in doing so. She was a desperate woman.

Why did the woman touch his garment?

A popularly held belief in Jesus' time was that the dignity and power of a person were transferred to the clothing he wore. This idea probably originated from a combination of instructions from Leviticus with quasi-magical notions widely held in that day.[7] (There is one other mention in the Gospels of an incident when touching Jesus' garment resulted in healing: people at Gennesaret begged Jesus that "they might just touch the fringe of His cloak; and as many as touched it were cured.")[8]

So God did allow for this kind of thing on a very limited basis. There was the danger, of course, that people would worship the article of clothing rather than the God who healed them. So it is not surprising we don't see this occurrence too often in Scripture.[9]

Every devout Jew wore a piece over his robe with four tassels on it. This was in obedience to Numbers 15:38–39: "They shall make for themselves tassels on the corners of their garments . . . to look at and remember all the commandments of the LORD." The woman most likely touched one of these tassels.

Why didn't everyone who pressed up against Jesus receive healing?

The crowd had been relentless in their zeal to be near him. Luke described the intensity of their pursuit with the same word used in other places for the squeezing action of a wine or olive press. Many hands touched Jesus, determined to get a blessing as he passed by. That is why the disciples reacted in disbelief when Jesus asked who touched him. Are you kidding? Who *didn't* touch you?

Though many reached out and touched him, only one was healed. In her moment of contact, something significant definitely happened. He felt power leave him; she knew instantly she was healed. But in light of the response of Jesus and the crowd, it seems no one else who pressed up against Jesus had this experience. Why?

Jesus gave us the simple answer. He told the woman, "Your faith has made you well." How much faith did she need? It didn't take much. As little as a mustard seed, Jesus once told his disciples. Faith is not viewed quantitatively in Scripture. It is a bit like being pregnant: either you are or you are not. You have it or you don't.

Her faith in him may not have been the ideal. Her belief may well have been mixed with common superstition. She probably could not have passed a theological exam or won any debates with the rabbis of her day. She simply believed in Jesus. And it was enough.

But while faith opens the conduit for the power of God to move, it is not the only prerequisite. God will move as he sees fit. Our belief that he will act in a certain way does not put him under some obligation to do so. "For My thoughts are not your thoughts, nor are your ways My ways," the Lord declares.[10] God will act according to his wisdom and purposes. He uses those acts to reveal his glory to the world.

In John 9:2–3 the disciples asked why a man was born blind, and Jesus answered, "So that the works of God might be displayed in him." God had a plan for the hemorrhaging woman that day. He arranged circumstances to intersect her life with the life of a twelve-year-old girl, moving miraculously in the course of one day to save both, and in the process send a message to the world.

He had even more in mind. He would reveal himself to this woman on a personal level as well, and she would leave that roadside changed in more ways than one. God planned to transform her entire life.

Why did Jesus insist on her publicly confessing her condition and healing?

Hadn't she suffered enough public scrutiny and rejection? Anyone who didn't know of her stigma would know it now. At first glance, it seems almost cruel to single her out from the crowd. But there was more going on here than meets the eye.

Jesus knew what the woman was thinking. Her understanding most likely contained misconceptions. She would have walked away from the scene of her miraculous cure knowing he had physically healed her. But her debilitating problem was so much greater than her physical condition. His intention was to make her whole.

The context of Matthew's account of the hemorrhaging woman leaves little doubt as to Jesus' purpose in calling her out of anonymity. Hers is one of three stories in Matthew 9 that highlight a combination of spiritual and physical healing. First, Jesus healed the paralytic. "Your sins are forgiven," Jesus told the man (spiritual healing). Then later Jesus told the man, "Get up, pick up your bed and go home" (physical healing). The second incident is that of the woman with the hemorrhage.

"Your faith has made you well," Jesus told the woman (spiritual). Matthew then explained, "At once the woman was made well" (physical). In the last incident, Jesus first asked the blind men, "Do you believe that I am able to do this?" (spiritual). Once they gave their assent, he touched their eyes and told them, "It shall be done to you [physical] according to your faith." Matthew was surely making a point by repeating this theme of holistic healing so many times in a row.

The physical problem may have been the driving need that brought each of these people to Jesus. Yet their need was so much greater. While they sought relief from their present physical suffering, Jesus came to bring healing that would save them from an eternity of suffering. He came to offer a relationship with him.

There was another misconception the woman held. She knew as she thrust her arm through the crowd that her touch would contaminate Jesus, making him ceremonially unclean. With his words, Jesus set her straight. "Go in peace," he told her. Guilt had no place in her healing. Rather than her making him unclean, he healed her of uncleanliness.

Jesus demanded a public confession for other reasons. He used her confession to verify her healing and declare her clean to the community, ending the disgrace of twelve years of social banishment. She could return to synagogue worship and resume relationships. No longer must anyone avoid contact with her. She was to be received and restored to her community.[11] Giving the woman the opportunity to publicly confess was in reality a gift.

Not only did he declare her clean to the crowd, but Jesus took the opportunity to publicly commend her faith. She and those around her needed to understand there was no magical power inherently contained in the fringe on Jesus' garment. He clarified it was her faith that had released God's healing power and made possible the cure, ruling out any other erroneous interpretations. It wasn't about a garment or touching him. It was about believing in him.

Why did the gospel writers intertwine her story with the Jairus account?

The three gospel writers sandwiched the hemorrhaging woman between two halves of Jairus's story. The simultaneous unfolding of these two events, along with the common language used for both accounts, seems intended to guide the reader to find significance in comparison.

Both Jairus and the woman were recorded as falling at Jesus' feet. Both were in desperate need and facing death. Both the woman and the little girl were identified as daughters, and in both cases their healings were immediate and complete. In spite of Mosaic law that warned against becoming contaminated either by touching someone with the woman's medical condition or a corpse, touch was integral to both healings: the woman touched Jesus' garment, and Jesus took Jairus's daughter by the hand. And in both accounts, faith was the catalyst for the miracle to occur. Jesus told the woman, "Your faith has made you well." He told Jairus, "Only believe, and she will be made well."[12]

One last striking similarity giving us insight is the contrast of faith and fear interwoven throughout both stories. The woman was terrified when Jesus called her to come forward and identify herself. The remedy for her fear was in trusting

Jesus. Matthew quoted Jesus as reassuring her: "Take courage; your faith has made you well."[13] Jairus was grief-stricken when his servants brought him the news of his daughter's demise even as he hurried Jesus to her bedside. Jesus quickly gave him a cure for his overwhelming fear: "Do not be afraid any longer, only believe."[14]

The intersection of these two stories has great significance, for the woman and for us, as we are about to see.

For Today's Woman

As the woman waited for Jesus to pass by, his progress was halted by the appearance of Jairus. The ruler of the synagogue was important and respected,[15] so it probably did not surprise her that Jesus would stop to listen to his request. Jairus's child was twelve years old, the same number of years the woman had been ill. The irony must have struck her as she listened to Jairus urgently plead for his daughter's life.

Might the thought have led her to compare her circumstances to the child's? Did she listen wistfully as the prominent town citizen begged in desperation? She was there on her own, fending for herself in an unsympathetic crowd. It must have been heart wrenching in light of her isolation to hear this father plead for help on his daughter's behalf. This little girl was so fortunate to be under the fierce protectiveness of such love! The woman's financial impoverishment must also have stood in stark contrast to the financial provision the child enjoyed in light of her father's livelihood. What a blessing to be a daughter of such a man!

She may have had such thoughts. Then after she was healed, Jesus insisted on speaking with her. And he stunned her by calling her *daughter*.

This is more significant than it might seem at first. Curious about how often Jesus used this word as an address, I searched for the term in all four Gospels. I was astonished to discover Jesus used it as a personal address *only this one time.*

The address may not have meant much to the crowd, but it meant everything to her. He had heard her thoughts. He wanted her to know she, too, was now someone's daughter. She had been adopted by the King of kings. Her Father was more important than a synagogue ruler. Her Father ruled the universe. She might be financially destitute, but his wealth exceeded anyone's. She was loved more passionately by her Father than she could have ever dreamed. His commitment to her would last for eternity. Her physical healing was just the beginning.

He offers the same to us.

In his letter to the Ephesians, Paul told us of God's kind intention: "In love, He predestined us to adoption as sons through Jesus Christ to Himself."[16] In the Greco-Roman world of Paul, adoption was a legal and permanent status change. The adopted child would have all of the rights and inheritances of a natural-born son. He was no longer liable for old debts, nor would he inherit from his natural father.[17] Paul surely had these parameters in mind as he used this metaphor to help his readers understand what they had been given in Christ.

A friend of mine experienced this relationship change firsthand. She and her husband decided to adopt a little girl from overseas. The process involved two separate trips to Russia: one to get the legal paperwork completed and meet their new daughter, and a second journey once the adoption was approved by the Russian government to get the four-year-old child and bring her home.

On the first trip, they spent as much time as possible with their little girl. She had been living in the orphanage for about a year after losing her mother. The couple bonded with the child immediately. The language barrier seemed not to matter as they spent time blowing bubbles and playing with her in the orphanage yard. My friend brought a picture book with photographs of her two sons and other extended family members to leave with the child to help her learn the names of her new family in their absence. It just about broke their hearts when the day came to depart. They left her with tears and fervent promises to return just as soon as they could.

Several months passed as they waited impatiently back in the States. Finally the day came when they received notice the adoption was approved. As quickly as it could be arranged, the couple made the journey back to the other side of the world. As they drove toward the orphanage, they worried that their new daughter would not remember them. What if she didn't want to go with them? Would she be willing to leave everything familiar to go to a new home?

As they approached the orphanage door, their little girl burst through it from the inside. "Mama! Papa!" she cried. And she rushed into their waiting arms. It was an unforgettable moment as all three cried tears of happiness that they were finally together again, this time for good.

As we listened to my friend recount the story days later,

I was awestruck with how much she and her husband had already fallen head over heels in love with this little girl. The bond between them was as strong as any natural parent has with his or her child. She had moved into the home and hearts of her new family and already had her two big brothers wrapped around her little finger. She was a full daughter and sister in every sense. Her parents would provide for her until she was an adult. Someday she would inherit one-third of her parents' estate along with her two brothers. Her rights and privileges as a family member were secure.

Paul's use of the adoption metaphor is a beautiful picture of the new relationship that we have with God. The relationship is permanent; it is a done deal. While the inheritance is in our future, the unbreakable family tie has already been made.

Like most adoptions, ours came at a great price. Our heavenly Father had a debt to pay before we could be legally his. We were in slavery to sin. His payment set us free and enabled us to become a part of his family. "You are no longer a slave, but a son," Paul wrote, "and if a son, then an heir through God."[18]

A house on the real estate market's value is pretty much determined by what someone is willing to pay for it. We can say the same for our worth. Our value has been determined by what God was willing to pay: the precious blood of Christ.[19] Our value to God is unfathomable. He proved it by paying an exorbitant, unimaginable price.

Just like the hemorrhaging woman, we receive healing power when he gives our lives his healing touch. It is the power of the Holy Spirit, who comes to dwell in us, infusing us with life and remaining in us as a guarantee of our future inheritance and redemption.[20] It is a power that will "do far more abundantly beyond all that we ask or think."[21] Just as he did for the hemorrhaging woman, who set her sights too low and focused on a physical healing, Jesus wants to do so much more in us than we can even imagine.

God is the perfect Father, constantly pursuing an intimate relationship with his children. He is never too busy to hear our concerns; there is nothing too big or too small to bring before him. He wants us to approach him boldly, and he will respond to us with compassion, patience, and love.[22] He is protective of our well-being and will supply all our needs.[23] He continually works in us, molding us into the best people we can be.[24] He disciplines us when we need it, always for our good, loving us too much to allow sin to lead us to our own destruction.[25] He will remain faithful forever, promising never to abandon us.[26] He truly is the perfect parent.

He calls us daughters. The truth of that and what it implies should overwhelm us as it did the hemorrhaging woman. His healing goes beyond what we could have even thought to ask. He has taken our guilt and washed us clean of its contamination. Our status has undergone a complete reversal. We are heirs to an amazing inheritance as adopted daughters of the King. Not one part of our lives remains unchanged.

After informing the woman of her new status, Jesus told her to "go in peace." For the first time in her life, she could do just that. Meeting Jesus and believing in him had changed everything. The peace she gained was a profound sense of well-being that could come only from a new relationship with God. No longer was he the God she must fear in light of her inadequacies and sin. Her salvation gave her the restoration she needed to pursue an intimate relationship with her heavenly Father. Her healing was complete.

❧ Food for Thought ❧

1. The hemorrhaging woman had narrow expectations about what Jesus could do for her. How have you limited your expectations of God in the past? How has he exceeded them?
2. How did this experience deepen your relationship with God?
3. What are the benefits of your adoption? (See Ephesians 1:5–14.) Which of these benefits is most meaningful to you?
4. Does knowing you are God's adopted daughter affect your view of yourself? In what ways?

❧ Journaling ❧

How should being an adopted daughter of the King affect your relationships with others? List the freedoms your new status has given you. List ways your interactions with others can reflect all you have been given.

chapter three

Now one of the Pharisees was requesting Him to dine with him, and He entered the Pharisee's house and reclined at the table. And there was a woman in the city who was a sinner; and when she learned that He was reclining at the table in the Pharisee's house, she brought an alabaster vial of perfume, and standing behind Him at His feet, weeping, she began to wet His feet with her tears, and kept wiping them with the hair of her head, and kissing His feet and anointing them with the perfume.

Now when the Pharisee who had invited Him saw this, he said to himself, "If this man were a prophet He would know who and what sort of person this woman is who is touching Him, that she is a sinner."

And Jesus answered him, "Simon, I have something to say to you."

And he replied, "Say it, Teacher."

"A moneylender had two debtors: one owed five hundred denarii, and the other fifty. When they were unable to repay, he graciously forgave them both. So which of them will love him more?"

Simon answered and said, "I suppose the one whom he forgave more."

And He said to him, "You have judged correctly." Turning toward the woman, He said to Simon, "Do you see this woman? I entered your house; you gave Me no water for My feet, but she has wet My feet with her tears and wiped them with her hair. You gave Me no kiss; but she, since the time I came in, has not ceased to kiss My feet. You did not anoint My head with oil, but she anointed My feet with perfume. For this reason I say to you, her sins, which are many, have been forgiven, for she loved much; but he who is forgiven little, loves little." Then He said to her, "Your sins have been forgiven."

Those who were reclining at the table with Him began to say to themselves, "Who is this man who even forgives sins?"

And He said to the woman, "Your faith has saved you; go in peace."

—Luke 7:36–50

Grateful Extravagance

___

JESUS AND THE SINFUL WOMAN

A woman emerges from the spectators at the banquet, anxious to express her love for Jesus. She washes his feet with her tears of gratitude and anoints him with expensive perfume. The host of the dinner is appalled. So why did Simon, an obviously antagonistic Pharisee, invite Jesus to dine in the first place? Did Jesus forgive the woman because of her ministrations? Or was there a message for woman and Pharisee alike in the words of Christ?

She was thrilled when she heard Jesus had remained in town. It was one more chance to see the man who had turned her world upside down. Stopping only to fill to the brim the small flask hanging from her neck, she hurried out the door to where Simon the Pharisee lived, just several blocks from her own home. Arriving breathlessly, she was not surprised to see fellow townspeople crowding around the entrance into Simon's courtyard.

She stood on the outskirts for a while, reluctant to push her way through the crowd. Finally she could stand it no longer. Taking a deep breath, unobtrusively as possible, she eased her way past those straining to listen toward the sound of the voice she had come to love. Most of those she brushed by had not much use for her anyway. She was known in these parts as a sinner, and any association with her meant the possibility of contamination. When she broke through the crowd, she found herself standing just a few feet from Jesus.

Like the other guests, he reclined at the low table, leaning on his left elbow, feet stretched out behind him. Glancing around the table, she caught the eye of their host. Simon silently glared at her, obviously signaling she was not welcome. The all-too-familiar sting of his disapproval and those of his ilk always cut her to the quick. But this day, she would not shrink from his judgmental opinion. She *needed* to be here.

Moving to stand directly behind Jesus, she suddenly hesitated. What could she say that would sufficiently convey her gratitude? Words were so inadequate to express the overwhelming love that flooded her heart. Tears blurred her vision as her fingers subconsciously closed around the flask hanging from her neck.

Jesus and his fellow guests were speaking animatedly as they dipped their bread into common bowls. Most of the disciples hadn't even noticed the unusual presence of a woman so close to the table, as engrossed as they were in conversation. The woman dropped to her knees. As she leaned over his feet, her tears fell freely, dropping onto his feet and running in rivulets through the dust that clung to him from the road.

Why were his feet so dirty? Hadn't his host provided for

him as they entered his home? Outraged at such scandalous neglect and rudeness, she again looked across the table to Simon, discovering that he continued to glare at her. *Let him stare*, she thought rebelliously. If he wouldn't provide his guest with even the most basic of courtesies, she would. Opening the flask, she poured the costly perfume onto Jesus' feet, gently smoothing the oil with her fingers and wiping them with her hair. Too emotional to speak a word, she kissed them, her tears continuing to fall unabated.

Simon watched the woman in disgust. He was not impressed. What holy man would allow a sinner like this woman to minister to him in this way? If he truly was a prophet, he would distance himself from her immediately. She was bad news and ought to be banished from their presence.

At that moment, Jesus turned to look behind him. His eyes lit with recognition as he watched her wipe the dust and tears from his feet with her hair. She continued to massage the oil into his feet, reassured by the warmth in his expression that he understood what she was wordlessly trying to convey.

Then Jesus spoke. While his eyes remained locked with hers, his words were for his host. "Simon, I have something to say to you," he said.

Simon straightened at his place. "Then say it, Teacher!" he replied.

Jesus turned toward him and began a story: "A money-lender had two debtors: one owed five hundred denarii, and the other fifty. When they were unable to repay, he graciously forgave them both. So which of them will love him more?"

Simon took a minute to answer. Was this a trick question, where the obviously correct answer was actually wrong?

"I suppose the one whom he forgave more," he cautiously responded.

Jesus nodded his head. "You have judged correctly." He gestured toward the woman, whose tears continued to flow as she repeatedly kissed and anointed his feet. "Do you see this woman? I entered your house; you gave me no water for my feet but she has wet my feet with her tears and wiped them with her hair. You gave me no kiss, but she, since the time I came in, has not ceased to kiss my feet. You did not anoint my head with oil, but she anointed my feet with perfume."

Simon dropped his gaze downward, embarrassed to hear his deliberate neglect as a host recounted out loud in front of all those in attendance. But with his next remark, Jesus demonstrated he was not being mean-spirited in pointing out Simon's gaffe. He was merely making a point.

"For this reason I say to you, her sins, which are many, have been forgiven, as her great love has shown; but he who is forgiven little, loves little." He turned to her and repeated the words he had spoken to her only earlier that day. "Your sins have been forgiven," he said boldly. "Your faith has saved you; go in peace."

A gasp rose from the crowd observing the dinner. "Who is this man that even forgives sins?" they whispered.

Her heart brimful of happiness, the woman placed one last reverent kiss on his feet and turned to go. This time as she moved through the crowd, they parted respectfully for her. Apparently she was to be labeled a sinner no more. Jesus had declared her clean. Peace flooded her heart. She was loved. She was whole. She held her head a little higher, her back a little straighter as she turned down the street. He had changed everything. She could barely keep herself from joyfully skipping the rest of the way home.

$\mathcal{D}$igging $\mathcal{D}$eeper

What is a Pharisee?

This incident is the only time Simon the Pharisee is mentioned in Scripture. His title identifies him as a member of the Pharisees, a religious and political party that enjoyed great power in first-century Israel. This group's roots went back to the time of the Maccabees, about one hundred fifty years before Christ, when conquering Seleucid King Antiochus IV set out to destroy the Jewish religion and way of life. In the ensuing revolt, a zeal for keeping the Mosaic law resurged. Two parties with a passion for the Law emerged from that movement: the Essenes, who broke away from Jewish society to live in isolated communities, and the Pharisees. The latter remained within Jewish society and were revered as the religious leaders of the Jews at the time of Christ.

While functioning as an active part of the Jewish community, the Pharisees did set themselves apart in many ways. In fact, their very name, *Pharisees*, means "separate ones." They were also known as the *Chasidim*, which meant "loyal to God."[1] The Jewish historian Josephus described them as "a body of Jews who profess to be more religious than the rest, and to explain the laws more precisely."[2] He estimated that there were approximately six thousand Pharisees in the first century.[3]

The Pharisees taught God's Word, instructing the people about how they were to live according to the Law. While much of their teaching was based on Mosaic law, there were many additional oral traditions firmly upheld as well. They confronted Jesus mostly about oral traditions, which he largely disdained. For example, Jesus and his disciples were chastised for failure to ceremonially cleanse their hands before eating.[4] This ritual was meant to wash away any uncleanliness resulting from contact with the general public, lest they symbolically contaminate their food and ultimately themselves. Jesus told them it was not what went into the mouth that made a man unclean, but the sin that already lies within. Another time, Jesus was reprimanded for allowing his disciples to pick grain from a field on the Sabbath.[5] Jesus retorted that the Pharisees' legalistic interpretation on keeping the Sabbath only added to the burden of man instead of granting the rest the Sabbath was meant to provide.

Purity was a big issue for the Pharisees. They would never touch the carcass of a dead animal or even anyone who had come in contact with one. Anyone who had been "defiled" through an illness was strictly avoided. In fact, the Pharisees limited their contact with any Jew who might fail to be as careful about keeping the Law as they were. Meals with the general public were especially suspect because there was no guarantee the food would be properly prepared and tithed. Therefore, a Pharisee would not deign to eat in the home of a non-Pharisee.

Such determination for stringent conformity to the Law had its pitfalls. The Pharisees' very relationship with God became about performing righteous deeds rather than loving God with all their hearts, souls, minds, and strength. The apostle Paul, once a Pharisee, summed up this kind of thinking: "Israel, pursuing a law of righteousness, did not arrive at that law. Why? Because they did not pursue it by faith, but as though it were by works."[6]

Since they defined holiness by how well one kept their rules, it was important for them to keep up appearances. The Pharisees excelled in putting up a good front. They wore special garments to distinguish themselves from the general public. They made sure people noticed when they gave to the poor, prayed, or fasted.[7] But as with any legalistic system, the proponents of the rules are as liable to fail as those they instruct. Jesus saw right through their pious preaching: "Do not do according to their deeds; for they say things and do not do them."[8] The old adage "Do as I say, not as I do" would readily apply to the Pharisees. For this reason Jesus called them *hypocrites*. It was a term usually used in that day for actors on a stage; it identified them as merely pretenders.[9]

Unfortunately the Pharisees failed to acknowledge this personal failure at holiness. They believed their virtue would earn them reward and a place in heaven. They had put God in a neat little box, defining his will by their list of dos and don'ts. But in their self-righteous zeal, they neglected what God wanted most: humility and repentance from sin. Jesus warned his disciples against that kind of "righteousness": "Unless your righteousness surpasses that of the scribes and Pharisees, you will not enter the kingdom of heaven."[10]

Although these issues seemed to be generally true for these religious leaders, there were certainly exceptions. Scripture notes three Pharisees who believed Jesus was the Messiah. Nicodemus, the Pharisee who questioned Jesus at night about being born again, most likely became a believer after that conversation recorded in John 3. (John mentioned that

Nicodemus assisted Joseph of Arimathea, also a pharisee-believer, in removing Jesus' body from the cross and provided the costly myrrh and aloes needed to prepare the body for burial.)[11] And as mentioned above, the apostle Paul, originally a Pharisee and even a son of a Pharisee, became a believer on the road to Damascus.[12]

We don't know whether Simon's encounter with Jesus led him to believe. He is not mentioned again.

Given his allegiance with the Pharisees, why would
Simon invite Jesus to his home for dinner?

It is difficult to get a read on Simon the Pharisee because his actions and thoughts are somewhat conflicting. On the one hand, Simon invited Jesus into his home for a meal. In view of the pharisaical restrictions on mealtimes, it is hard to believe that he would dine with someone he considered impure. He also called Jesus "Teacher," the equivalent of Rabbi, a title of respect. In addition, his astonishment that Jesus welcomed the attentions of the sinful woman belayed his assumptions that Jesus would act as any holy man set apart for divine service would, at the least avoiding contact or ordering her away.[13] Furthermore, Simon seemed to have initially debated about whether or not Jesus was a prophet, a possibility that he eliminated when Jesus seemed unaware of her sinful status. All of these points seem to indicate a man who had not made up his mind about this young preacher.

On the other hand, Simon's actions indicated a certain amount of disdain toward his guest. In first-century Judaism, hospitality was a sacred responsibility. Simon's serious breach of the laws of hospitality was an affront to the honor of his guest, something normally guarded by the host at all costs. Social convention demanded a host greet his guests with a kiss of peace, one hand warmly placed on the guest's shoulder. Cool water was to be provided to allow the guest to cleanse his feet of the dust of the road; this was considered a minimal courtesy. A few drops of oil were to be placed on the guest's head before he entered the dining area. All of these things, normally expected of any host, were neglected at this dinner. The failure to show honor was an unspoken insult and could be construed as an attempt to belittle those whom Simon entertained that evening.

So why *did* Simon invite Jesus into his home? There are several possibilities. He might have wanted to satisfy his curiosity. With his preaching and miraculous signs, Jesus had created quite a stir in the Galilean region. Simon could have wanted a chance to evaluate the man up close for himself. It is also possible Simon wanted to actively discredit Jesus, using the opportunity to find some word or action that could be used as a charge against him.[14] After all, the Pharisee party as a whole was anxious to rid themselves of this thorn in their side. Finally, a self-serving motive might have been at play. There would be a certain prestige in entertaining someone who was on the rise to celebrity status. The Pharisees were all about appearances, remember. Having Jesus in his home would have given Simon a feather in his cap when it came to social status.

Whatever his initial motivation, Simon got more than he bargained for. Jesus moved him right past the surface and into the very heart of the matter. Appearances were not the issue. It was all about the heart. Love like the woman expressed came only as a result of forgiveness and an intimate relationship with God. As Jesus pointed out these things, Simon must have inevitably observed the contrast between her lavish, deeply emotional attentions and his own callous disregard. It was an unexpected opportunity for him to see his shallow attempts at holiness and discover his great need for forgiveness.

If Simon considered the woman a sinner, why was she able to attend the dinner?

In first-century Middle Eastern culture, members of the general populace were welcome to stop by a dinner when a visiting rabbi was invited, so they could listen to his teaching and the ensuing conversation.

The homes of well-to-do people were conducive for this kind of gathering. They were constructed with large central courtyards, and during the warmer months dinners would be eaten there. The table would have been low to the ground. Invited guests would recline on low couches or pillows, their upper bodies close to the table, and feet stretched out behind them. Bystanders who came to hear the conversation would have walked up and gathered on the periphery of the invited guests.

While women had begun to attend such gatherings in the Greco-Roman world at large, the feeling persisted in Israel that their presence was generally inappropriate.[15] The sinful woman's presence at Simon's banquet would have been unusual and most likely frowned upon.

Who was the woman?

Luke informed us that she was a "sinner." That label had a broad-reaching scope. More than just prostitutes, sinners were those who had frequent associations with Gentiles. Tax collectors, who worked for the Romans, for example, were labeled as such. Even people who experienced a serious illness or disability could be branded as sinners with potential to contaminate those around them.[16] (It should be noted that Luke did not utilize the word *sinners* for people with illnesses in other places; he did not label the hemorrhaging woman, for example, as a sinner.)

So while we know that the Pharisees and townspeople thought of her as a sinner, we don't know why. Somehow, whether it was a life spent in something as dramatic as prostitution or an occupation less damning, we know from Luke's label she had experienced a certain level of rejection by her community.

In the sixth century, Pope Gregory the Great taught that this woman was a prostitute and even identified her as Mary Magdalene.[17] Since that time, the Catholic Church has altered its position on this teaching.[18] But the idea persists to this present day.

Was she wealthy? Her possession of an expensive alabaster vial indicates she probably was a woman of some financial means. Women without brothers could inherit from their fathers.[19] Or she might well have worked for a local employer or even owned a personal business. Women in the Greco-Roman world are recorded as having worked as weavers, doctors, hairdressers, attendants, and musicians.[20] If she was married, she and her husband may have labored together in a family business, as did Priscilla and Aquila.[21]

It is likely Simon's dinner party was not the first time the woman had encountered Christ. After all, Jesus told Simon that her actions were an expression of gratitude for forgiveness she had already received. Furthermore, Jesus told her, "Your sins have been forgiven." He used the perfect tense of the verb, which in the Greek expresses a past action whose effects endure into the present.

If she had already been forgiven, why did Jesus declare her forgiven again?

What Jesus said to the woman seemed unnecessary, since she was already acting in response to her faith. But Jesus was speaking with the onlookers in mind, giving those around him an insight into his identity. In the Old Testament, God alone had the authority to forgive sins. By saying what he did, Jesus was claiming deity.[22] This was not lost on either Simon or the crowd gathered in his home. If his claim was not true, Jesus was guilty of blasphemy, a crime punishable by death. If it was true, he was none other than the Son of God.

A second reason Jesus may have publicly declared her forgiven was that the town needed to know of her new status before God. Whatever the reason, she had previously borne the stigma of sinner within her community. By publicly declaring her forgiven, Jesus was giving her a fresh start.

Luke's literary structure seems to confirm this. In verse 48, Jesus told the woman her sins were forgiven. In verse 50, he told her that her faith saved her. These verses stand like parallel bookends, surrounding verse 49.[23] In verse 49, Luke told us the crowd wondered, *Who is this man that forgives sins?*

Jesus was taking the opportunity to clarify what saved her. It was not her act of anointing his feet. It was not her tears, for they were about gratitude, not about contrition. It was her faith. Her relationship with God was changed because she believed in Jesus. And that decision to trust in him opened the conduit for God's grace to transform her. In a room full of people striving to earn God's favor, this clarification needed to be voiced out loud.

For Today's Woman

The woman's extravagant actions were appropriately fitting, for she offered them in response to something extravagantly given to her: grace. Grace is unmerited favor. You cannot earn grace—it's undeserved by definition. The forgiveness she had received was in no way a reward for her actions. It was given in unconditional love.

Not only was it unmerited, but it was also unlimited. Scripture describes the grace of God using words like *abounding*, *abundance*, and *surpassing*—and tells us God *lavished* his grace upon us.[24] Like a fountain spilling over, God's grace is a source that will never run dry. Paul wrote the Romans that "where sin increased, grace abounded all the more,"[25] assuring us that we cannot overwhelm or out-sin grace. Whatever we have done, God's grace is bigger.

We like to classify sin, making careful distinction between the minor and the major ones. It's what the Pharisees did. They couldn't be sin-free, so they drew lines in the sand. Some sins were condemning, others forgivable. They picked and chose what was acceptable and what was not. But no sin is acceptable to God.

Remember, Jesus' parable was about not one but *two* debtors. They *both* owed quite a sum. A denarius was equivalent to a day's earnings. Therefore one debtor owed two months' wages, the other two years'. Inability to pay either debt would have landed a person in jail.

One summer, as a program leader at camp, I was given the responsibility to review the testimonies of girls desiring to be baptized. One sweet little girl had carefully written out her experience with Jesus Christ. She had been raised in a Christian home and had become a believer at a young age. "I've never done any of the really bad sins," she assured me. I was interested in this statement. What were the really bad sins? "Like murder, stealing, or adultery," she replied.

I took her to James 2:10: "Whoever keeps the whole law and yet stumbles in one point, he has become guilty of all." Had she ever lied or hated someone or disobeyed her parents? Of course she had. She was human. I tried to break the news gently: that she was guilty of it all. The Bible never quantifies guilt. You are guilty or innocent. One or the other. In the Bible, there are no shades of guilt.

Fortunately for us, guilty as we are, a pardon is offered through no merit of our own. "Through one act of righteousness there resulted justification of life to all men," Paul wrote the Romans.[26] Jesus' death on the cross provides payment for sin. One man's act makes those who believe in him righteous. The heavenly Judge bangs his gavel and proclaims the guilty now innocent. The captives are set free.

God's grace is lavish. It accomplishes what our most sincere and stringent efforts never could. The scope of its magnitude is beyond what we could ever do that might threaten its effectiveness. It is given, not in remuneration, but in spite of what we've done. *Extravagant* is a perfect word to sum up the width, depth, and height of the grace of God.

The woman's actions on the evening of Simon's dinner may well have seemed extravagant, even inappropriately so to some witnessing the scene. But they were most definitely appropriate to what she had been given. Jesus moved her from sinner to saint, rejected to accepted, condemned to free. In her mind, she couldn't do enough to express her gratitude.

Too often we consider our acts of worship akin to a to-do list. We should daily have our morning devotions, spend a few minutes in prayer, and maybe perform some good deed toward our neighbor. Our agenda looks more like an inventory of obligations than the grateful response of the sinful woman. If that is how we think, then our mind-set resembles Simon's a lot more than hers. God isn't looking for obligatory righteous acts. He wants our hearts.

Go in peace. It's what Jesus told the woman when she finished her anointing and turned to leave. I was curious about how often Jesus used that particular send-off. A perusal of the Gospels revealed he said it to just one other person: the woman with the hemorrhage who touched his garment to be healed. Why to just these two women?

They had something in common. Both were living lives of condemnation and isolation; the "sinner" because of her lifestyle, the hemorrhaging woman because of her ailment. They were unacceptable to society at large, avoided in fear of contamination via contact. Both came to Jesus desperate to be "well," and he declared both of them healed: the hemorrhaging woman of her twelve-year ailment, and the sinful woman of her deplorable status. Both had been transformed from unclean to clean. Both were commended for their faith.

So he urged them to *go*, begin to live lives that reflected their new relationship with God. This could happen because something was very different after their encounter with him. Their hearts were finally at peace. They had peace with God, and due to Jesus' public declaration, they could enjoy peace with their neighbors. The stigma had been removed, all barriers to relationships destroyed.

Jesus had changed everything for the sinful woman. Unfortunately not so for Simon, who seemed to have missed the point. In his pharisaical lifestyle, he was a living checklist of dos and don'ts. He didn't get that while she was most definitely a sinner, he was one too. His blindness to his spiritual need made him feel self-sufficient: he thought to earn favor with God his way. But Simon and his fraternal society of Pharisees had it dead wrong. Only a sense of need could open the door for forgiveness. Only a confession of helplessness would make the way open for grace.

Jesus told the Pharisees he had come to heal the sick.[27] We are all sick—some of us just don't recognize it. But whether we sense the spiritual sickness inside us or not, it is growing and will eventually destroy us without the intervention of healing grace. The first step in healing for any illness is recognizing the symptoms and acknowledging we are in trouble. Only then will we seek the Great Physician. Only then can he make us well.

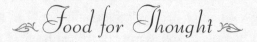

Food for Thought

1. Jesus identified the brand of religion that the Pharisees promoted as hypocrisy. Read Matthew 23:24–28. List the word pictures

Jesus used in that passage to describe their outrageous behavior. What does each picture convey about the Pharisees?

2. Are pharisaical actions and attitudes present in the church today? Can you think of specific examples when you have seen hypocrisy in your place of worship? What are the damaging consequences for promoting this kind of morality in the body of Christ?

3. Is it possible to guard against hypocrisy? List the ways you are personally guilty of putting up a false front. How can you avoid falling into the trap of hypocrisy in the future?

4. The Pharisees condemned certain sins and ignored others. Do you tend to do the same? (For example, do you view abortion or homosexuality as being on the same level with lying or gossip?) What might motivate us to create a false dichotomy of sin? (See Rom. 3:23 and James 2:10 for God's view on sin.)

❧ *Journaling* ❧

The sinful woman's effusive actions at the banquet demonstrated her great love and gratitude for what Jesus had done for her. List the ways you are grateful to him for what he has done in your life.

Jesus is no longer physically present, so we can't kiss his feet or anoint him with costly perfume. What can we do to express our love and gratitude, now, in the twenty-first century? How can we respond to the grace we have received? List several practical ways you can demonstrate your feelings with action.

chapter four

Jesus went away from there, and withdrew into the district of Tyre and Sidon. And a Canaanite woman from that region came out and began to cry out, saying, "Have mercy on me, Lord, Son of David; my daughter is cruelly demon-possessed." But He did not answer her a word.

And His disciples came and implored Him, saying, "Send her away, because she keeps shouting at us."

But He answered and said, "I was sent only to the lost sheep of the house of Israel."

But she came and began to bow down before Him, saying, "Lord, help me!"

And He answered and said, "It is not good to take the children's bread and throw it to the dogs."

But she said, "Yes, Lord; but even the dogs feed on the crumbs which fall from their masters' table."

Then Jesus said to her, "O woman, your faith is great; it shall be done for you as you wish." And her daughter was healed at once.

—MATTHEW 15:21–28

(THIS STORY IS ALSO RECORDED IN MARK 7:24–30.)

Adding Insult to Injury?

JESUS AND THE SYROPHOENICIAN WOMAN

A desperate mother approaches Jesus, begging deliverance for her precious little girl. At first, Jesus seems to be completely unresponsive to her pleas—is he rudely ignoring her? Then, when he finally does talk to her, he compares her to a dog under the dining table, begging for crumbs. How could he treat her so unkindly? What was really going on?

*A*s she hurried along the road, the woman barely noticed the beauty of the harbor. The sounds of fishermen and merchants calling to each other as they loaded or unloaded their boats did not register with her; her mind was on one thing only. She was on her way to seek an end to her little daughter's demon possession.

The man she sought that day was a Jew from Galilee. His name was Jesus, and his reputation had preceded him into Syria. Word was he had healed the sick and even raised the dead. Most important to her, she'd heard stories of his casting out demons. Now he was in her town. For the first time in a long time, she dared to hope that help was possible. The child's self-mutilation and erratic behavior were frightening to anyone who witnessed them. Like any mother would, she desperately sought deliverance before the demon eventually destroyed her daughter.

As the woman neared the house, her footsteps slowed. She began to have second thoughts about his willingness to help. She knew the Jews labeled anyone who was not Jewish a Gentile. She also knew well the disdain with which Jews regarded all Gentiles. How would this Jewish man receive her? Somehow she must convince him that despite racial barriers, her cause was worthy of his attention. Anyone with a heart would surely not turn his back on a desperate mother. She raised her fist to pound on the door.

The men on the other side of the door reclined around the front room in exhaustion. It had been an emotionally draining few weeks. The most recent days had been a blur of healings, teachings, and miracles. Everywhere they went, crowds pressed in on all sides, clamoring for just a touch of Jesus' garment. The group finally left Israel in a desperate quest for anonymity. Every man yearned for just a few days of peace and quiet. Suddenly a loud knock sounded, disturbing the calm of the house.

One of the disciples let her in. It was unusual and considered inappropriate for a woman to approach men outside her home. She knew her brazenness would make all those inside ill at ease. She quickly ascertained which one was Jesus as several of the men rose to form a protective human barrier around him. Seeing the expressions on the men's faces and sensing an imminent rejection, she lost no time in expressing her request. The strong emotion in her shaking voice plainly revealed the desperation in her heart.

"Have mercy on me, Lord, Son of David," she cried. "My daughter is cruelly demon-possessed." A heavy silence greeted her plea. Not easily dissuaded, she repeated herself, crying out again and again for her little girl's deliverance.

Clearly uncomfortable with this woman and her emotional tirade, the disciples impatiently waited for Jesus to respond. While his face looked weary in the dim light, he did not seem impervious to her pleas. He gazed at her with understanding and compassion, which surprised none of them. Never had they seen Jesus refuse to answer someone who so humbly pleaded for his help.

Yet for the moment he remained silent. And as she continued to beg loudly, the disciples grew increasingly uneasy. Finally one of the disciples could take it no more. "Jesus, send her away. She keeps shouting at us," he complained.

Jesus looked from the woman to focus on his exasperated disciples. This was a teachable moment. And they had much to learn. He had recently clarified God's idea of clean and unclean food for them. Now, by entering Tyre, he planned to eliminate the distinction between clean and unclean peoples.

Yet the disciples were not the only ones harboring a misconception. Jesus had not missed the fact the woman had called him "Son of David," thus exclusively identifying him as the promised Savior of Israel. She had no idea she and her people needed him to be their Savior as well.

69

Unexpected Love

Two very different perspectives, one Jewish, one gentile, both arriving at similarly misguided convictions. Jesus was about to blow their faulty ideas away. As he finally spoke, Jesus appeared to be answering his disciples. But his words were carefully chosen for her as well. "I was sent only to the lost sheep of Israel," he said.

The disciples seemed satisfied with Jesus' response. They were all too ready to dismiss this desperate mother and get on with their respite. Yet while the disciples might have been unfazed that Jesus would reject her, the woman was not so easily deterred. Shamelessly she fell to the ground, lowering her face to the floor at Jesus' feet. "Lord, help me," she begged. She could not accept no for an answer.

Jesus turned away from his disciples and looked straight at the woman. He extended his hands and gently assisted her to her feet. As she lifted her eyes to meet his, what she saw filled her with hope. Contrary to the censure his recent words seemed to indicate, there was not rejection in his gaze, but kindness. Her heart began to pound as he directly addressed her for the first time.

"It is not good to take the children's bread and give it to the dogs," he told her.

The woman considered his statement carefully. She understood what he meant. The head of Israel's house was their God. He provided for his children, the Jews. They were his top priority.

Yet she also knew the God of the Israelites was unlike any god worshipped in Tyre. The Israelites claimed their God, while powerful, cared deeply for his people. Surely a God with that kind of character would want to help an innocent child,

70

Gentile though she might be. God's mercy, even the leftover mercy, would be enough.

She made use of Jesus' metaphor in her response. "Yes, Lord," she agreed. "But even the dogs feed on the crumbs which fall from their masters' table."

At her thoughtful and passionate response, Jesus broke out in a broad grin. Her answer brimmed full of trust in God alone. "Woman, your faith is great," he told her. "It shall be done for you as you wish."

With a heart filled with gratitude, she departed. Upon her arrival at home, the woman found Jesus was true to his word. The demon had been banished from her daughter forever. She was completely healed.[1]

Digging Deeper

What do we know about the Syrophoenician woman?

Mark identified the woman as Syrophoenician. Matthew called her a Canaanite. Are these labels in conflict with each other? Not at all. Each writer had his specific audience in mind as he penned his gospel account.

Matthew was writing to the Jews. His identification of the woman as a Canaanite would have struck a chord with his original readers. The term was actually quite antiquated by the first century. This is the one and only time the word appears in the New Testament! Using it in the first century would be akin to us in this century referring to the Danes as Vikings.[2] So why did Matthew use it?

Canaanite was an ancient label identifying the eclectic

mix of peoples who inhabited the land between Egypt and Asia Minor. Their pagan culture was one of sexual idol worship and gross immorality.[3] The Canaanite-Israelite relationship was acrimonious from its earliest days. Matthew knew his readers would have immediately perceived this woman as an enemy, an ethnic and religious outsider, by labeling her as he did.

Mark's identification tells us she was a Phoenician by race, living in Syria. The Phoenicians were a people known for their advanced accomplishments in sailing and the first written phonetic alphabet. The people of Tyre also took great pride in being a historic center for the worship of many deities, regularly practicing idol worship, pagan rites, and polytheism.

The vocabulary Mark used in his account also indicates she was a woman of means, since she returned home to find her daughter on a couch, as opposed to a mat, which suggests a higher level of affluence than most people of the time.[4]

Was Jesus insulting the woman when he compared her to dogs under the table?

The fact that Jesus compared the Gentiles to dogs under the table can be a bit disconcerting if you are unaware of the vocabulary nuances in the original language. There are two Greek words for dog. One is a word for the dogs that wandered the streets; Jews commonly used this word as an insulting label for Gentiles. To the Greek, this word also meant a shameless and audacious woman. In English we have a curse word that echoes a similar sentiment, which also means a female dog.[5]

However, Jesus used a different word, more literally translated "little dog" or "puppy." It described a household pet or a lapdog. To the Greek, this diminutive term would be an affectionate one.[6]

We need to remember that Jesus was using a metaphor here. It was a word picture meant to convey an idea. We should not look for a literal correspondence to true life in the objects he chose. For example, if I described my husband as a treasure chest of knowledge, you would not think his head was a wooden box that sported actual hinges and a lock. You would naturally understand I am conveying the idea of a precious cache of information he has stored away in his memory.

Jesus was not calling the woman a dog. He was using a word picture to bring to mind the popularly held idea that God would work only on behalf of the Jews. He would soon move the woman and his disciples toward understanding that this assumption was misguided.

Jesus chose to use this particular metaphor only when speaking with a Gentile. Jews of the first century typically disdained the idea of having a household pet. Gentiles, however, commonly had pets. A Jew would have had a much different emotional reaction should someone compare him to a dog.[7]

Was Jesus reluctant to heal the woman's daughter because she was a Gentile?

Was Jesus responding in a way that was racially prejudiced? This is impossible for several reasons.

First, to reject someone because of race would be sin. James defined this for us very clearly in his epistle: "If you show partiality, you are committing sin and are convicted by the law as transgressors. For whoever keeps the whole law and yet stumbles in one point, he has become guilty of all."[8] Since Scripture clearly informs us Jesus was without sin, racial prejudice could not be true of him.[9] In addition, Jesus himself had Canaanite ancestry in his blood. Matthew recorded two women, both of Canaanite descent, who were a part of the direct genealogy of Christ: Tamar and Rahab.[10] Finally the Syrophoenician woman was not the first Gentile to benefit from the healing ministry of Jesus. In Matthew 8, he healed a Roman centurion's servant. In Mark 3, Gentiles from Tyre and Sidon are also examples.

Jesus knew God's offer of salvation would be extended to Gentiles as well as Jews. He reveals this when he said, "I am the good shepherd, and I know My own and My own know Me. . . . I lay down My life for the sheep. I have other sheep, *which are not of this fold; I must bring them also, and they will hear My voice;* and they will become one flock with one shepherd."[11]

Why, then, did Jesus seem to separate the Gentiles and the Jews with his metaphor in regard to receiving favor from God?

In each of his encounters with people, Jesus began his conversation right where they were. The woman believed him to be Israel's Messiah, calling him "Son of David." The disciples believed the same, that the Gentiles had no claim over their Messiah. The metaphor Jesus used at first seems to confirm their assumptions. But the woman quickly found the hole in the logic: even while the children were still eating, the dogs could be fed also. By articulating their belief, Jesus was helping those in the scene think through the implications of their convictions. There is no limit to the mercy and grace of God.

What light does the context shed on this encounter?

Matthew preceded this account with another: a confrontation between Jewish Pharisees and scribes over the failure of Jesus' disciples to follow tradition. They had failed to ceremonially clean their hands before eating, a custom prescribed in the Mishnah. This scribal practice required holding the hands under running water up to the wrists. It was not a matter of hygiene; it was a ritual to ceremonially clean away anything a Jew might have touched that day. If the hands touched an unclean thing, then touching food that entered a person would make the entire person unclean.

In response to their accusation, Jesus redefined the traditional view of uncleanliness by pointing out that "it is not what enters into the mouth that defiles the man, but what proceeds out of the mouth, this defiles the man."[12] Being unclean was a condition that existed within a person, due to the sinful nature of the entire human race. He later explained to his disciples: "The things that proceed out of the mouth come from the heart, and those defile the man. For out of the heart come evil thoughts, murders, adulteries, fornications, thefts, false witnesses, slanders. These are the things which defile the man; but to eat with unwashed hands does not defile the man."[13] Rather than arising from merely outward causes, uncleanliness was a state of the heart.

It was a new concept of defilement. Now as if to drive the point home, both gospel writers next chronicled Jesus' trip outside the boundaries of Israel, unclean territory by Jewish standards. During this Syrian visit, Jesus first encountered the Syrophoenician woman. Next Jesus spent time healing the sick among the Gentiles of the region. Then Jesus miraculously provided a meal for a crowd of four thousand Gentiles with seven loaves of bread and a few small fish. The gospel writers seemed to be making a point with these incidents placed carefully together. Before the trip, Jesus first dismissed the distinction between clean and unclean foods. Then by entering gentile territory, he dismissed the distinction between clean and unclean peoples. All stood in need of a Savior. Faith alone would save them from the consequences of their sinful state. Faith alone could jump the boundaries that race had erected.[14]

Another interesting clue is found in the surrounding context of Matthew 15:1–16:12; every scene described somehow includes bread. Eating bread without ceremonial cleansing was the subject of the pharisaical confrontation at the beginning of the chapter. The gentile crowd of four thousand was fed bread. In chapter 16, the disciples were concerned that they did not think to bring bread. Jesus turned their concern about physical bread around and warned them to beware of the leaven of the Pharisees and Sadducees.

In Scripture, bread is used figuratively for food or sustenance in general.[15] Jesus referred to himself as the Bread of Life in John 6:49–59. As food is necessary to physical life, Jesus is necessary to spiritual life. In the tabernacle, the shewbread indicated the presence of the Lord. At Communion, we take the bread as a symbol of the body of Christ, given over to death that we might have life. Why did Jesus use the example of bread with the Syrophoenician woman? While the woman was at first interested only in getting deliverance for her daughter, Jesus brought up the idea of bread with the woman. He was interested in more than her daughter's immediate physical need. He was opening a discussion on the woman's spiritual need for eternal life as well.

In the miraculous feedings of thousands, there were always leftovers; many baskets of bread and fish were collected after everyone had eaten his fill. The Syrophoenician woman claimed the leftovers for the Gentiles. Divine provision for Israel can be extended to the Gentiles, and Israel will not experience any lack. There is enough mercy from God to go around.[16]

For Today's Woman

The Syrophoenician woman stands in stark contrast to the religious leaders portrayed in the verses preceding her story. The Pharisees demanded an explanation from Jesus about why his disciples did not follow accepted ceremonial practices. Jesus responded by confronting them on a way they had neglected a command from Mosaic law: honoring their fathers and mothers. He saw beyond their pious, religious façade straight to their proud, hypocritical hearts.

Although loud and maybe even inappropriate in her cries, the Syrophoenician woman never came close to arrogance or self-sufficiency. Every word she spoke, every action we see, confirms her humility and total dependence on the mercy of Christ. The Syrophoenician woman beautifully and clearly portrays the first step of faith: admitting helplessness and unworthiness. She acknowledged no claim to the Jewish Messiah. She understood that he was under no obligation to her. She knew how the Jews viewed the Gentiles. She knew she had no place breaching the domain of men and presumptuously putting her request before him. Yet she went anyway, placing herself at his mercy, falling at his feet in total submission and desperation.

She did not list a bunch of reasons why Jesus should honor her request. She did not talk about what a bright or well-behaved child her daughter was. She did not tell about her excellent mothering skills or how she had lived a good life. Although it is very possible her economic status would have given her standing in the community, not one mention was made of it as she spoke to him. It was never about her accomplishments. It was all about the mercy of Jesus.

Women today have worked hard to prove themselves in the marketplace. We have advanced degrees and are dedicated to our careers. There is a certain pride in what we have accomplished. We have learned to stand on our own two feet, no longer the perceived helpless housewives of the 1940s and 1950s.

We may be tempted to approach God with that kind of self-sufficient mind-set. But God is not looking for what we have accomplished to give his approval. He is looking for a heart ready to trust in his goodness. He wants us to look past our surface accomplishments to inside, where our faults and needs reside.

When we dare to be honest with ourselves, we know we fail to meet the standard of a completely holy God. We understand when it comes to spiritual matters, we are truly lacking. Nothing we have accomplished could ever make up for the sin we have committed or the damage we have done. None of us is worthy to stand in the presence of God.

When Jesus brought up the metaphor of the puppies eating bread meant for the children at their masters' table, the Syrophoenician woman did not flinch. She stood her ground, fully accepting her less-than-worthy status. She never pretended to be anything but a gentile woman coming to beg Jesus for help.

God wants us on these same terms. He wants us to see honestly who we are. He wants us to admit our sin, our faults, and our weaknesses. Only when we are honest in our self-evaluation is he free to come in and make a difference in our lives. God's greatest work is done through our weakness. Paul expounded on this idea in his letter to the Corinthians when he recalled the words of Jesus: "My grace is sufficient for you, for power is perfected in weakness."[17] Our understanding of our helplessness is an integral part of our relationship with him. We must understand he is the Vine, the Life-giver and Sustainer. Without him, we can accomplish nothing.[18]

In Revelation we read of a church that had the opposite attitude. It was located in the prosperous first-century town of Laodicea. Christ spoke to this church: "You say, 'I am rich, and have become wealthy, and have need of nothing,' and you do not know that you are wretched and miserable and poor and blind and naked."[19] The Laodiceans were rich, all right. They were rich in self-sufficiency and pride. Yet in their arrogance they had missed the point: they were living in spiritual poverty.

The city of Laodicea was a great commercial and financial center. It was famous for manufacturing a soft, glossy black wool, popular in local and export trade. Banking was a strong industry in the city. Laodicea also boasted a well-known medical school that developed several medicines. One in particular was a salve used to cure eye diseases. Christ offered his church in Laodicea spiritual counterparts to these things: "Buy from Me gold refined by fire so that you may become [truly] rich, and white garments so that you may [truly] clothe yourself, and that the shame of your nakedness will not be revealed; and eye salve to anoint your eyes so that you may [truly] see."[20] They were poor, naked, and blind. Only what Christ offered could truly solve their need.

We need to pay careful attention to these two examples given to us in Scripture: one positive, one negative. The Laodiceans had it all wrong. In their self-sufficiency, they were unacceptable to Christ. The Syrophoenician woman, on the other hand, hit the bull's-eye. She understood her unworthiness. She threw herself on the mercy of God.

And Jesus commended her faith.

It is important to note that Jesus did not commend her persistence. He did not commend her humility. These were only external evidences of her faith. They were not what captured his attention. Her faith was the thing. She trusted in his power and goodness. She knew he could make her daughter well. So without blinking an eye, she heard his metaphor and responded appropriately. And Jesus loved her response.

The Syrophoenician woman trusted Christ. Because of her belief in his power and mercy, she made herself vulnerable, risking rejection and censure by even daring to approach him. And her faith was commended as better than all of Israel's.

❧ Food for Thought ❧

1. How do you relate to the Syrophoenician woman? Can you put yourself in her shoes? Do her desperation and resulting actions tug at your heart?

2. Compare the disciples' actions in this story with Matthew 19:13–15. What do you think motivated the disciples to be so protective of Jesus?

3. Jesus told the Syrophoenician woman: "Because of this answer go; the demon has gone out of your daughter" (Mark 7:29). What was it about her answer that pleased Jesus? What do you learn from the Syrophoenician woman's example about how to pray? For further insight, read 2 Chronicles 7:14; Luke 18:1–8; and James 4:10.

4. The Syrophoenician woman was banking on God's having enough grace and mercy to go around. In Ephesians 1:7–8, Paul told us the riches of God's grace have been lavished on us. Peter told us to prepare for action by fixing our hope completely on God's grace (1 Peter 1:13). In addition to enabling your salvation, how does the abundance of God's grace affect you in the here and now as you seek to live for him?

5. When Jesus left Israel and traveled into Tyre, he extended his invitation to follow him to the Gentiles. This was no doubt confusing to his disciples, who understood the Messiah to be exclusively for the Jews. After Jesus' ascension, Peter was given a vision to confirm God's plan to include the whole world in his offer of salvation. Read Acts 10:9–29. How do you think Jesus' encounter with the Syrophoenician woman retrospectively added to the disciples' understanding of God's plan?

✍ *Journaling* ✍

How does the faith of the Syrophoenician woman compare to how you relate to God? Make a list of the components of her faith that you can find revealed in Matthew 15:21–28 and Mark 7:24–30.

Are you ever tempted to try to earn God's favor? Make deals with him in an effort to manipulate him into granting your request? What does the faith of the Syrophoenician woman reveal about this kind of thinking? Write a letter to God, confessing the times you have succumbed to trying to earn grace. Tell him how you plan to change your intercession in the future.

chapter five

Everyone went to his home. But Jesus went to the Mount of Olives. Early in the morning He came again into the temple, and all the people were coming to Him; and He sat down and began to teach them.

The scribes and the Pharisees brought a woman caught in adultery, and having set her in the center of the court, they said to Him, "Teacher, this woman has been caught in adultery, in the very act. Now in the Law Moses commanded us to stone such women; what then do You say?" They were saying this, testing Him, so that they might have grounds for accusing Him. But Jesus stooped down and with His finger wrote on the ground.

But when they persisted in asking Him, He straightened up, and said to them, "He who is without sin among you, let him be the first to throw a stone at her." Again He stooped down and wrote on the ground.

When they heard it, they began to go out one by one, beginning with the older ones, and He was left alone, and the woman, where she was, in the center of the court. Straightening up, Jesus said to her, "Woman, where are they? Did no one condemn you?"

She said, "No one, Lord."

And Jesus said, "I do not condemn you, either. Go. From now on sin no more."

—JOHN 7:53–8:11

Fork in the Road

JESUS AND THE ADULTEROUS WOMAN

Dragged through the streets, thrust onto the floor of the temple courtyard, the woman caught in adultery awaits her fate. Ready to condemn her, the Pharisees demand a sentence from Jesus. But a darker motive than justice is afoot. Why does Jesus entertain their question when they are clearly out to discredit him? Why do her accusers react the way they did to his answer? How would Jesus' words have affected the woman still shaking on the floor?

She could barely keep her wits about her as her captors jostled and pushed her down the narrow street. Everything happened so fast. Just minutes before, they burst into the room where she lay half-asleep in her lover's arms, shouting their condemnation and outrage while she frantically scrambled for her clothing. With no apparent interest in her partner, the men roughly grasped and dragged her out the door. Now they hurried her down the streets, their intent unmistakable. She was being taken to the temple.

Those within the temple gates stepped aside to allow the angry group entrance. Their curious stares and whispered questions as she passed shamed her as much as the condemnation of her captors. The group reached the courtyard. There she was thrust onto the ground and left for all to see, shaken, weeping, guilty. The morning sun glared down on her head as she tried to straighten her garments and somehow make herself presentable. Looking up, she saw her accusers move toward a young rabbi who was teaching a small group on the outskirts of the courtyard.

Jesus stood up from his seat on the steps as they approached. One of the scribes began to speak, his voice loudly echoing against the smooth stone walls: "Teacher, this woman has been caught in adultery, in the very act." A gasp of outrage arose from bystanders watching from the perimeter of the courtyard. "Now in the Law, Moses commanded us to stone such women," the scribe continued. "What then do *you* say?"

The woman saw the other scribes and Pharisees leaning forward for his answer. All of them seemed to have forgotten she was even there as they focused on the teacher. She did not understand. Why was he being consulted? Who was he? Was this all the trial she would receive?

As if to separate himself from the leaders in their condemnation, Jesus stooped down and began to write something in the sand on the temple's stone floor. She could not see what he was writing. But she saw the anger of the Pharisees grow as they watched him, indignant at his lack of response. They were important men and usually enjoyed reverent respect from their fellow Jews. Not easily dissuaded, they continued to demand an answer. Should the woman be stoned in punishment for her sin?

Finally Jesus straightened. He calmly eyed each one in turn as he spoke. His words were simple but carried great weight: "He who is without sin among you, let him be the first to throw a stone at her." Then he stooped back down and resumed writing with his finger.

Trembling, feeling sick to her stomach, the woman waited to see who would begin the execution. Once the first stone had been cast, they would all join in. Tears streamed down her face. She didn't want to die.

No one moved. The courtyard went silent. Seconds turned into minutes as each man contemplated Jesus' words. The eldest of the group was first to respond. He turned and simply walked through the courtyard exit. Soon another older man quietly followed him. One by one the Pharisees and scribes quietly left the scene. Even the uninvolved spectators slipped away. It wasn't long before she and Jesus were the only ones left.

The woman shakily rose to her feet, unsure of what to do next. Jesus stood up once more. He came over to where she stood. "Woman, where are they?" he gently asked. "Did no one condemn you?"

She shook her head in disbelief. "No one, Lord," she said.

He nodded. "I do not condemn you, either. Go. From now on sin no more."

Digging Deeper

***How does this encounter fit with the message of the
Gospel of John?***

Unfortunately, while context is usually most helpful in
finding the best interpretation of a passage, it is not in this
case. Your translation of the Bible may feature a notation on
John 7:53–8:11 that indicates it is not found in the earliest
manuscripts. What does this mean?

We do not have the originals of the writings that comprise
the New Testament. We do have copies of them, which were
meticulously handwritten and passed from church to church.
The oldest of these date to the early second century, some less
than one hundred years after the originals were composed.
They are impressively accurate copies: when compared, even
those dated many years apart are very consistent, with only the
occasional insignificant discrepancy, like a differing article or
preposition. It is obvious those who had the responsibility to
do the duplication took their job very seriously.

The earliest of these copies do not contain this story of the
adulterous woman. This means one of two things: either the
story was added later (and not by John), or the story was originally in the gospel and taken out by a copier who felt it too
controversial. Many scholars argue the language is dissimilar
enough to the rest of the gospel that John was not the author.[1]
They also feel that the story, rather than contributing to the
general flow of John's account, is actually an interruption.
Contrarily there are scholars who feel this passage is consistent
with the rest of John's gospel and find no basis to deem it anything other than John's composition.[2]

In later manuscripts, when the story begins to appear, it is not always in John 8. Some have it after John 7:36, after 7:44, or tacked on to the end of John's gospel. It is sometimes even found in Luke!

Therefore, putting importance on the immediate context of this story does not make sense, since there is no clear "home." Yet we cannot dismiss the account entirely because it rings true in its characterization of Jesus and the Pharisees with the rest of the Gospels. Because it may have been added later does not mean the story is untrue. For that reason, we will treat this passage with the same consideration as the other conversations between Jesus and women. But we will not place great import on the context in John 8. Instead we will use the general context of the four Gospels to assist us in drawing conclusions.

Why did the religious leaders really take the woman to Jesus?

The writer made it plain that the scribes and Pharisees who took the woman to the temple had more on their minds than seeing a cheating wife punished for unfaithfulness. He revealed in 8:6: "They were . . . testing Him, so that they might have grounds for accusing Him." Their motive was calculated: catch Jesus saying something that might be used against him.

That was becoming a common occurrence in the ongoing relationship between Jesus and the religious leaders. From the early days of his ministry, the Pharisees considered Jesus a threat and conspired to have him eliminated. For example, early in his gospel, Mark told us they conspired with the Herodians about "how they might destroy Him."[3] Later in

Mark, we read of the Pharisees and Herodians attempting to entrap him with another tricky question: "Is it lawful to pay a poll-tax to Caesar?"[4] To affirm Rome's right to tax the populace would have angered potential followers, who hated their Roman oppressors. To deny it would have put him in serious trouble with the local Roman authorities.

Jesus wasn't fooled for a minute. Their question was not an honest inquiry. He did not take the bait. Instead, he pointed out the likeness of Caesar imprinted on a coin. "Render to Caesar the things that are Caesar's, and to God the things that are God's," he replied.[5]

Now, on this morning, they were attempting the same ploy. No matter what Jesus answered, they figured he would discredit himself.

What was the dilemma Jesus faced?

The controversial issue was punishment for adultery. In Jesus' day, Rome allowed the Sanhedrin (a Jewish supreme court comprised of Pharisees, Sadducees, and scribes) the power to govern the Jews in Judea.[6] However, Rome alone reserved the power to inflict capital punishment.

That created the conflict. The law of Moses prescribed a death sentence for those caught in the act of adultery.[7] In Roman law, however, adultery did not warrant the death penalty.[8] To affirm Roman restrictions would essentially be speaking against the law of Moses. On the other hand, to uphold Mosaic law and its death penalty would be insurrection in the eyes of Roman authorities.[9] It seemed no matter how Jesus answered, he would be pulled into conflict, either with the Romans or with the Jews.

Another evidence of dark pharisaical motives can be found in their selective indictment. In Mosaic law, both the man and the woman in an illicit sexual relationship were equally guilty and should suffer an equal punishment. Deuteronomy 22:22 reads: "If a man is found lying with a married woman, then both of them shall die, the man who lay with the woman, and the woman."

They claimed to have caught her "in the very act" of adultery; this meant both lovers were present at the time of discovery. So then why was she alone being hauled through the streets and into the court of the temple? If their intent truly was to uphold Mosaic law, they were holding up only half of it. The conspicuous absence of the woman's partner indicates a likely double standard and seems to signify disingenuousness on the part of her accusers.

Why, then, did Jesus entertain the question?

Knowing their intent did not keep Jesus from giving them an answer. Jesus was concerned for each person in that courtyard. The writer who recorded the incident demonstrated this in his structure of the story: both accusers and accused are dealt with in parallel fashion.[10] Both interactions, first with the Pharisees and then with the woman, began with Jesus stooping to write in the sand. His words to each were a pronouncement about sin. He was offering each a chance to turn away from his or her sin.

Jesus intended to use this incident in a momentous way for all those involved.

First, there was the woman. Had Jesus refused to answer, in their anger the mob might have turned on the woman and lynched her, even in light of Roman restrictions.[11] (Not long after this incident, Stephen was stoned by the Sanhedrin for his message about Jesus recorded in Acts 7.) Jesus' intervention on her behalf very likely saved her life.

Until Jesus spoke, the woman's treatment by the religious leaders had been abominable. They regarded her as merely an object to be used to suit their malicious purposes. Her fate, her very life, mattered not at all to the Pharisees. Jesus set out to show her a different way: God's way.

Please realize: the Old Testament makes it clear there is judgment for sin. God is holy, and sin would not be allowed to run rampant in his people. But there was a huge difference in the judgment handed out by God and the condemnation of the Pharisees. God's judgment serves a purpose: to bring the sinner to repentance.

Read through any of the Prophets and you will find harsh warnings for those who have rebelled against God. Yet interspersed with those dire warnings are promises of blessing and peace for those who listen to the word of God and turn away from their current path. God's ultimate desire is not to destroy, but to restore. He is not willing that any should perish.[12]

The Pharisees, on the other hand, had no goal of redemption. There was nothing constructive about their dealings with this woman. They had already condemned her, written her off. Moving her toward restoration hadn't even crossed their minds.

So the Pharisees needed to be shown God's way as well. They regarded themselves as holy, spending their lives carefully observing the Law, both Mosaic and oral traditions. As far as they were concerned, they were clean and had the right to stand in judgment of others. Their thinking was nothing short of delusional. They desperately needed a reality check!

Whether they knew it or not, the Pharisees were not much different from the woman. All were guilty of sin in their lives. All needed forgiveness. All needed a personal relationship with God. So Jesus took the opportunity to urge each one of them toward redemption. He answered them: "He who is without sin among you, let him be the first to throw a stone at her."

Why did the Pharisees react the way they did to Jesus' answer?

Jesus was not suggesting anything new to the Pharisees. His answer came straight out of Mosaic law, something they already knew. Deuteronomy dictated that those who provided testimony against the sinner were to be the very ones to initiate a stoning: "The hand of the witnesses shall be first against him to put him to death, and afterward the hand of all the people."[13]

There was a grave responsibility in being witnesses to the sin of adultery. Their words would very likely lead to someone's death. If they gave anything but honest testimony, the witnesses would have blood on their hands.

Deuteronomy also commanded: "If the witness is a false witness and he has accused his brother falsely, then you shall do to him just as he had intended to do to his brother [that is, put him to death]."[14] If the Pharisees had done anything to entrap the woman so that they could challenge Jesus, then by law, they were putting their own lives at risk.

A story written in the period of time between the Old and New Testaments would have been very familiar to anyone in Jesus' day. It was the account of beautiful Susanna, the wife of a rich man of Babylon, who was falsely accused of adultery. The witnesses were two men who actually attempted to force sexual relations on her, but she resisted and called for help. When the servants responded to her alarm, the men made up a story of seeing her engage in adultery with a younger man.

Since the men were elders in the community, the court assumed their testimony valid and condemned Susanna to die. However, before the sentence could be carried out, a discerning young man named Daniel questioned the two elders separately and found a discrepancy in their stories that proved they were lying. The assembly responded in horror that innocent blood had nearly been shed. They quickly put the two elders to death for their false accusation.[15]

Knowing the story, knowing the Scriptures, and then hearing Jesus' words, those who were ready to testify against the woman would have been stricken with fear. Any false motive, any false statement, could possibly backfire should their dishonesty come to light. It is very likely that a need for self-preservation won over the desire to entrap Jesus.

So they cut bait and left.

Did his words of enlightenment eventually bring any of the accusers to repentance? We'll never know. There are only a few Pharisees who are named in Scripture as becoming followers of Christ.

What did Jesus write in the sand?

The Bible doesn't tell us what Jesus wrote. Was he drawing mindless doodles? Probably not. The Greek verb used here, *graphō*, refers to letters or words. What words might Jesus have written?

Was his silent scrawling intended to convict the Pharisees with God's Word? Could he have written out Exodus 23:1: "You shall not bear a false report; do not join your hand with a wicked man to be a malicious witness"? Or maybe Proverbs 19:9: "A false witness will not go unpunished, and he who tells lies will perish"?

It is easy to picture the Pharisees peering over his shoulder as he scratched the letters into the sand, gradually being filled with consternation as the full reality of what they were attempting to do hit them.

Of course, all this is complete conjecture. The writer didn't inform his readers of the words Jesus wrote or mention that the Pharisees ever read them. But it is interesting to think about the possibilities.

Why would Jesus instruct the woman to "sin no more"?
Isn't that impossible?

If at some point in your life you have ever tried to stop sinning for good, Jesus' command to the adulterous woman probably causes you to wonder.

At the moment of salvation, we receive more than eternal life. God initiates a remarkable transformation within us: our very nature is changed into something completely different. Paul called it a "new creation."[16] What exactly has changed? We possess a new capability. Before Christ, we had no inherent ability to have a relationship with God.[17] Our minds were hostile toward him.[18] We could not understand spiritual things.[19] Our hearts were darkened, and we loved the darkness rather than the light.[20]

Receiving a new nature opened up a new horizon for us.

We now have a brand-new potential to live in an intimate relationship with God. Our new nature makes it possible to understand spiritual truth.[21] We were given more than the light of knowledge—we were flooded with the love of God as his Spirit came to dwell within us.[22]

That new potential extends to our will, affecting our ability to choose between right and wrong. While we once were helpless under the power of sin, we are powerless no longer.[23] We have the capability of turning away from the temptation of sin and living our lives in a manner consistent with our commitment to God. In short, with our new nature, God equipped us with everything needed to live within his will.[24]

It remains a battle, to be sure. While each of us has been set free from the slavery of sin and made a new creation in Christ, the new nature coexists with the old flesh and its corrupted desires. It will be a struggle until we leave the old nature behind to dwell with God in eternity.[25]

Yet while the struggle continues, our general direction has changed. He is moving us toward something we never could have accomplished on our own. He is at work in us to complete the transformation he started when he saved us. He is changing us into the image of Jesus Christ.[26]

The Connecticut River flows from north to south through the heart of New England. If you were to get into a canoe somewhere between Vermont and New Hampshire and allow the current to move you, you would eventually find yourself in the Long Island Sound. But if you consulted a compass while on the journey, a southward progression might not always seem evident. At times, you might be moving in an eastward or westward direction. Sometimes you might even be headed northward! But no matter how it may appear at any given moment, the general direction of the river's flow would bring you ever southward and to an eventual arrival at Long Island Sound.

Like the Connecticut River, our lives are moving in a general direction. While we often struggle with sin, our course has been altered as believers. God is at work in us to bring our new potential into a reality. And that transformation process will continue until the day of Christ Jesus.[27]

Christ was calling the woman to step onto that new path. It was an invitation to turn away from her former lifestyle and walk in newness of life. He was offering a new beginning, a chance to leave her sordid past in the dust. If she chose to follow him, nothing would ever be the same again.

For Today's Woman

Jesus' concern for the adulterous woman stood in stark contrast to the lack of concern shown to her by the Pharisees. To them she was a throwaway, a mere pawn in a plot to discredit Jesus. It really didn't have much to do with her at all. To the Pharisees, it was nothing personal.

With Jesus, it was very personal. It has always been that way with God. He doggedly pursues a relationship with each of us, one on one. As God told Moses, "You have found favor in My sight and I have known you *by name*."[28]

The Atlantic coast is just two hours away from where I live. The weather, wave height, and water temperature can vary greatly with each visit to the shore. But one thing remains a constant at the beach. It is the presence and pervasiveness of sand. Sand is between your toes as you walk and crunches between your teeth as you eat your picnic lunch. Copious amounts of it travel home with you no matter how carefully you brush off the cooler or shake out the blankets and towels. Yet as much as you might inadvertently take away, you won't make a dent in the vast amount remaining on the beach.

David compared the unimaginable number of grains of sand in this world to the number of thoughts God had about him:

> *How precious are your thoughts about me, O God!*
> *They cannot be numbered!*
> *I can't even count them;*
> *they outnumber the grains of sand!* [29]

Can you imagine how many grains of sand exist? God's thoughts of us are more numerous than a beach full of them!

His thoughts go beyond an amazing quantity; they are startling in how individually personal they are as well. Whether we are aware of his presence or not, he is involved even in the very mundane details of our lives. Jesus told his disciples that "the very hairs of your head are all numbered."[30] David wrote that God knows

> *when I sit down and when I rise up;*
> *You understand my thought from afar. . . .*
> *[You] are intimately acquainted with all my ways.*
> *Even before there is a word on my tongue,*
> *. . . You know it all.* [31]

It should not surprise us that Jesus, the exact representation of God's being, should be so purposefully personal.

One of the ways we see this demonstrated is his approach that individually addressed the particular needs of each person he encountered. His interactions began right where they were. He aimed right for the heart with the truth they needed to hear. He used their specific circumstances to draw them into a relationship with him, changing their lives forever with a single encounter.

The adulterous woman was no exception.

Before she met Jesus, the woman's concept of God and his standards most likely involved a long list of dos and don'ts. Her understanding had come either directly or indirectly from the Pharisees. They were the teachers of the Law; the brand of Judaism that people believed in and practiced then was significantly shaped by pharisaical thought.

Unfortunately these leaders believed in performing to the letter of the Law, but their attempts at holiness never reached into their hearts. They might have been meticulous in following ceremonial procedure, but pious acts could not erase their guilt. Jesus enlightened them with his charge to them to self-examine. Their newfound revelation was enough to quiet the angry mob and make them walk away.

In seeing this, the woman surely began to understand sin in a new light. It was not eliminated by righteous acts. Everyone, religious leader and adulterous woman alike, is equally guilty of sin. In her encounter with Jesus, she realized true righteousness was not earned by pious behavior.

Once she grasped that truth, Jesus moved her to the next necessary understanding: Forgiveness could come only by grace. Facing him alone in the courtyard, she was without hope of restoration. She could do nothing to pay restitution for her sin, nothing that would earn forgiveness. So his next statement must have been most unexpected. "Neither do I condemn you," he told her. Jesus was offering what neither she nor anyone could ever deserve. Unmerited favor. He was offering her grace.

Now she stood at a fork in the road. And Jesus knew it. So he gently urged her in the direction she ought to go.

He did the same for one of his disciples. Peter was reeling from abysmal failure. Despite his good intentions, he had succumbed to fear and denied Christ. He had failed the test. It was a fork in the road. Either Peter could allow the weight of guilt to incapacitate him, making him effectively useless for the kingdom, or he could move forward into the work that Jesus had prepared him to do.

After his resurrection, Jesus sought out Peter and several disciples on the beach at the Sea of Galilee. They enjoyed a breakfast of freshly caught fish together. Then Jesus took Peter aside. "Simon, do you love me more than these?" he asked.

Peter expressed his sincere remorse and passion for Jesus with a simple response. "Yes, Lord, you know I do," he answered.

Jesus pointed him forward. "Tend my lambs," he commanded. Three times Jesus asked the question. Three times Peter affirmed his love and commitment, one for each time he had denied Christ. Jesus was helping Peter put his recent failure behind him and move forward into the work of kingdom building.[32]

He is interested in doing the same for us. There will be

times when we come upon a fork in the road. Maybe circumstances in our lives make a sudden change. Or he gives us a startling revelation, some insight that demands a response. We stand uncertain at the crossroads, wondering where to go from here.

Jesus is the same personal Savior he was to the adulterous woman shivering in the courtyard. He knows where we are and where we need to go. His desire is to see us transformed, changed from the inside out. He offers us grace and direction. His path is ours to choose.

Paul wrote the Philippians: "Forgetting what lies behind and reaching forward to what lies ahead, I press on toward the goal for the prize of the upward call of God in Christ Jesus."[33] *Go. Sin no more.* God has removed our condemnation and guilt. He has plans for our transformation. It's time to look ahead. It's time to move forward.

Food for Thought

1. At our salvation, God placed us on a new path headed in a new direction. As illustrated by the Connecticut River, we can make twists and turns in our lives that may disguise our general direction. Think about your life now compared to last year. How has God changed you? What evidence is there that you have moved in a positive direction? What has he taught you about himself that you didn't know last year?

2. The Pharisees were eager to judge the adulterous woman. The problem with sitting in judgment is that we are also guilty. Is it wrong to recognize the sin in others? No. The Holy Spirit in us

alerts us to the presence of sin. But in our response to that knowledge, we must also be sensitive to his leading. Read Galatians 5:22–23. List the fruit of the Spirit. How should each of them temper our response to the sin of another? List practical examples next to each fruit.

3. Our response to the sin of another should always have restoration as its goal. See Galatians 6:1–2. What do these verses teach you about the attitude that will be most helpful in accomplishing this?

4. Rather than dwell on your sin or the sin of others, where should your attention be focused? Read Hebrews 12:1–3. What instructions does the writer give that will keep your gaze where it belongs? What are practical ways you can implement these commands in your daily life?

⨳ *Journaling* ⨳

"Neither do I condemn you. Go. Sin no more". With these words, Jesus was giving the adulterous woman an opportunity for a new life. She was completely forgiven for her sins. It was a chance to start over.

He offers the same to us. But while we gratefully accept the idea of grace, we often stubbornly carry the baggage of guilt for our past over into our new life. Does God want us to continue to wallow in guilt? Read Micah 7:19; Psalm 103:10–14; and Romans 8:1–2. What is God's view of our sin?

Do you harbor guilt even though the guilt of your sin has been removed? List the things in your past you continue to feel guilty about. Then, in big, bold letters, write the words of Psalm 103:12 over the list with a marker. Thank God that Jesus made full payment for these things on your behalf. Then ask him to remove the burden of your residual guilty feelings. Write out Jesus' invitation: "Come to Me, all who are weary and heavy-laden, and *I will give you rest . . .* For My yoke is easy and My burden is light."[34]

chapter six

Now as they were traveling along, He entered a village; and a woman named Martha welcomed Him into her home. She had a sister called Mary, who was seated at the Lord's feet, listening to His word. But Martha was distracted with all her preparations; and she came up to Him and said, "Lord, do You not care that my sister has left me to do all the serving alone? Then tell her to help me."

But the Lord answered and said to her, "Martha, Martha, you are worried and bothered about so many things; but only one thing is necessary, for Mary has chosen the good part, which shall not be taken away from her."

—LUKE 10:38–42

Misery Wants Company

JESUS AND MARTHA

Hot and sweaty from her work in the kitchen, Martha explodes when her sister deserts the meal preparation to go and sit with Jesus. Jesus' reply to Martha's indignation surprises her. Was he commending Mary for shirking her duties? Criticizing Martha for trying to serve him? Since when did serving become a bad thing?

For the tenth time that afternoon, Martha peered out the front window. She was beside herself with excitement. Jesus was coming, due to arrive any time. Determined to do everything possible to honor him in her home, Martha had spent two days in preparation for the dinner. All was in order. The table was ready, cushions placed around its perimeter to provide a place for her honored guests to recline. Goblets stood in a row waiting to be filled with the finest wine. The fragrance of freshly baked bread permeated the air. Clean water and towels for the travelers to wash their dusty feet had been placed near the door. Mentally ticking off what was needed to welcome Jesus into her home, Martha reassured herself she had thought of everything.

At long last, the group arrived. Lazarus, Martha, and Mary welcomed Jesus and his disciples with warm enthusiasm. After washing their feet, the guests entered the room prepared for the meal. Martha hurried into the kitchen to finish the last-minute cooking and food preparations. There was so much to think about! She moved from tabletop to hearth and back again. Delicious aromas filled the air as the meat quickly browned and crackled in the grease. She began to dish out the first course into bowls. Suddenly she did not have enough hands. Everything was ready to be served at once. Where was Mary?

Martha peeked her head into the dining room. To her surprise, Mary appeared to have abandoned her! She had seated herself near Jesus, actually participating in the lively discussion. Martha was horrified. What did she think she was doing? A lone woman seated among men, infringing on their conversation? What would Jesus think?

Her anger grew as she thought of all she had done to make this evening perfect. Jesus was well known in these parts. The miracles he had performed were the talk of the town. His remarkable and authoritative teachings had created quite a stir among religious leaders and laypeople alike. When Jesus accepted their invitation, Martha was determined everything would be perfect. She had spared no expense, shopping carefully for the best meats and vegetables in the village market. She was locally known for her hospitality. She wanted this meal and the time spent at her home to be beyond anything Jesus had experienced.

Now there was her sister, not only neglecting to help her, but sullying the evening by her disregard for acceptable behavior. A woman had no call to sit where Mary was sitting! What Jesus must be thinking! After all Martha had done, slaving away to make this night special, Mary was ruining it all.

Watching her sister animatedly discuss the kingdom of God with their honored guest, Martha felt more than scandalized. She felt betrayed. She had worked so hard, and her sister was treating the presentation of the meal as if it didn't even matter. There was so much to be done in these last few minutes, and there was Mary, reclined like there were servants to wait on her and their guests. Hot, sweaty, and incensed at her sister's disregard for her labor, Martha boiled over.

"Lord," she blurted out, abruptly interrupting the conversation. Jesus looked up, as did the disciples. Mary seemed almost surprised to see Martha in the doorway. Really? Had she forgotten all that still needed to be done in the kitchen? Had she not even a thought for her poor sister slaving away over the hot fire while she sat in comfort? Apparently not!

"Don't you care that my sister has left me to do all of the work? Alone? Would you please tell her to get into the kitchen where she belongs and help me?" Standing in the doorway, Martha's eyes shot daggers at her sister, who blinked in reaction to her angry, self-righteous tone. Arms crossed, Martha waited to hear the Lord put Mary in her place.

"Martha, Martha," Jesus said gently. "You are anxious and troubled about so many things. But really, only one thing is necessary. Mary has chosen the good part, which will not be taken away from her."

Digging Deeper

Where did Martha go wrong?

To be honest with you, as a woman, this story has always rankled me. I am not alone. Many women, I find, share my reaction. Was Jesus actually criticizing Martha for working in the kitchen? Was he really commending Mary for abandoning her sister to finish dinner preparations alone?

The traditional interpretation of this account I have always heard goes something like this: Martha was wrong in allowing her meal preparations to keep her from worshipping at Jesus' feet. Mary had the right idea: it is so much better to rest at Jesus' feet than to be busy serving. Martha: bad. Mary: good. We all need to be like Mary and not let our doing get in the way of our worship.

But Scripture does not seem to support this interpretation. In the first place, hospitality is a God-given mandate. In the Old Testament, it is included in Mosaic law: "The stranger who resides with you shall be to you as the native among you, and you shall love him as yourself."[1] Many Old Testament saints, like Abraham and Lot, took seriously the responsibility for the care and protection of guests. When accused of sin, Job used a claim of hospitality as a proof of innocence: "The alien has not lodged outside, for I have opened my doors to the traveler."[2] Isaiah offered hospitality as a way that Israel could demonstrate repentance:

> *Divide your bread with the hungry*
> *And bring the homeless poor into the house. . . .*
> *Then you will call, and the LORD will answer.*[3]

Even God is pictured as the ultimate host:

> *You prepare a table before me in the presence of my enemies;*
> *You have anointed my head with oil;*
> *My cup overflows.*[4]

In light of this, Martha surely viewed her service as obedience to a scriptural directive. Therefore, it must have come as a shock when the Lord chose Mary's actions over hers as the "good part." The original Greek reveals she expected an affirmation from him.[5] But Jesus did not back her up as she expected.

In the second place, the importance of serving pervades the Gospels. Again and again Jesus urged an attitude of servanthood to his disciples, who were often guilty of vying for the most influential spot in the coming kingdom of God. "If anyone wants to be first, he shall be last of all and servant of all," he told them.[6] In fact, the very nature of Christ's coming was an act of selfless service: "The Son of Man did not come to be served, but to serve, and to give His life a ransom for many."[7] Living life in imitation of a Servant-king necessitates our willingness to serve as well. Jesus defined the members of his family as those "who hear the word of God and do it."[8]

The practical implications of the traditional interpretation also shed doubt about its validity. If Martha dropped everything then and there and joined Mary at Jesus' feet, just how in the world was dinner going to get on the table? After all, he and his disciples relied on the hospitality of others as they traveled from town to town preaching! Since when did service suddenly become a bad thing?

What would this world look like if we all became Marys, sitting around being "spiritual" and letting everything around us fall apart?

Women are champions at getting things done. We are the movers and shakers on every church committee. We keep our families, households, and workplaces running. As the old song goes, we bring home the bacon *and* fry it up in the pan. So it is offensive to think Jesus would cast aspersions on all that, implying service is far less spiritually valuable than Bible study, prayer, or contemplative thought.

Rather than drawing us closer to Jesus, the traditional interpretation suggests a God who assigns responsibility to serve and then disapproves of us as we do it. It just doesn't ring true, from a scriptural viewpoint or in light of common sense.

So what was Martha's problem?

Since Jesus viewed service as integral to following him, it does not make sense that he would criticize Martha for serving him that evening rather than sitting at his feet. So what *was* he getting at with Martha?

"Martha, Martha, you are worried and bothered about so many things," he observed. Those two words, *worried* and *bothered*, give us insight into Jesus' point. He was not commenting on Martha's service. He was commenting on her mind-set. Rather than comparing listening and serving, Jesus was comparing anxiety and anger with figuratively sitting at his feet in peace.

The first word, *worried*, is the Greek verb *merimnao*, often alternatively translated as "to be anxious." Jesus used the same word later in Luke when he told his disciples, "Do not worry about your life, as to what you will eat; nor for your body, as to what you will put on. . . . For all these things the nations of the world eagerly seek; but your Father knows that you need these things."[9] Jesus knew anxiety would be detrimental to service. He wanted his disciples free from that distraction.

The second word, *bothered*, is the Greek verb *thorubazo*, which means "to be troubled, disturbed, or disquieted." It was most commonly used in reference to an angry crowd in a state of uproar or riot.[10] Martha had gotten herself all worked up. She was up to her ears in anxiety-induced anger.

It hadn't started that way. Luke told us that Martha welcomed Jesus into her home. That word, *welcomed*, appears only one other time in Luke, in the story of Zaccheus. Zaccheus, a much despised tax collector, wanted to see Jesus, who had extraordinarily taken on another tax collector as a disciple. So he climbed a tree in an effort to spot Jesus from above the crowds. To his amazement, Jesus stopped right under his tree and looked straight up at him. "Zaccheus, hurry and come down, for today I must stay at your house," he said. Zaccheus could hardly believe it. The most hated man in town was being singled out by the great teacher. With much joy, he welcomed Jesus into his home and life.[11]

This second context of this word usage suggests a welcome characterized by enthusiasm and helps us characterize the kind of welcome that Jesus got from Martha. It was a joyous reception. She was delighted to have him in her home, thrilled at the chance to serve him a meal at her table. So when did things go sour? How did Martha morph from gracious hostess to indignant victim?

I have to conclude that in all the excitement, Martha lost her perspective. She began to focus on the service rather than the one she served. And everything fell apart.

It's what happens when we get off center. We may start with an altruistic motive. We see a need and want to fill it. But if our service does not come out of our love for God, it is likely doomed to become all about us. As we serve, we easily slip into seeking a sense of significance from what we are doing rather than finding it in our relationship with him. Craving even greater satisfaction, we begin to look around and compare ourselves with others, eventually turning our service into a platform for judgment. Why aren't they doing what I am doing? Or why don't they do it my way? The service becomes "our baby," something that defines us and our meaning, and it is not about God at all.

We can imagine Martha starting a slow burn as she stirred the food on the hearth. She had slaved away all day long. No one appreciated how hard she was working. Mary had left her to shoulder the whole meal, thoughtlessly seating herself at Jesus' feet; that this was socially unacceptable behavior only added to Martha's anger. By the time she surfaced in the dining room, Martha's slow burn had developed into a raging fire. Her condemning outburst said it all. Martha had lost her perspective.

What exactly was Jesus commending Mary for choosing?

"Mary has chosen that good part, which will not be taken

away from her," Jesus told Martha. A look back at the larger context of this story will be helpful in determining exactly what the good part is. The gospel writers were very purposeful in how they grouped stories together, often using proximity to illustrate a point. Observing Luke's strategic placement adds valuable insight into our interpretation of Jesus' words.

Earlier in Luke 10, Jesus sent out seventy disciples in pairs to prepare selected cities for his future visit. They returned from their assignment flushed with victory. "Lord, even the demons are subject to us in Your name!" they exclaimed.[12]

Jesus rejoiced with them, but cautioned them as well. God had given them great power. But power tends to corrupt. If what they were doing became their focus and reason for being, their ministry would cease to be about bringing glory to God. It would become all about them: their works, their success, their fame. "Do not rejoice in this, that the spirits are subject to you, but rejoice that your names are recorded in heaven," he warned them.[13]

In other words, don't lose sight of why you are in ministry in the first place.

In response to these words, a teacher of the Law asked him to elaborate about getting one's name recorded in heaven. "Teacher," he asked, "what shall *I* do to inherit eternal life?"

Jesus asked him, "What is written in the Law?"

Answering that was a no-brainer for any teacher of the Law. He rattled off Deuteronomy 6:5, the Shema, a familiar creed to any Jew, along with a portion of a verse in Leviticus.[14] "You shall love the Lord your God with all your heart, and with all your soul, and with all your strength, and with all your mind; and your neighbor as yourself," he added.

"You have answered correctly," Jesus affirmed. "Do this and you will live."[15] Jesus was basically reiterating the concept he had just spoken to the excited disciples. A relationship with God is the Main Thing. It all boiled down to faith, to loving God and trusting him. Service was a secondary, natural outflow of that wholehearted love for and devotion to him.

The lawyer wanted specifics. "And who is my neighbor?" he asked Jesus.[16]

In response, as he often did, Jesus told a parable to illustrate what service motivated by a love for God would look like: the story of the good Samaritan.[17] A man had been robbed, beaten, and left for dead on the roadside. Two religious leaders callously walked right by him. Finally a Samaritan came by. Of anyone, he would be least likely to stop, for Jews hated the Samaritans. Yet the Samaritan came to the man's rescue. He administered first aid and then left him in an innkeeper's care, promising to doubly reimburse any expenses the man incurred until he was able to travel again.

The good Samaritan performed his service with no thought of personal benefit or reward. It wasn't about him at all. Loving your neighbor as yourself has its foundation in the first of the commands the teacher of the Law quoted: loving the Lord your God with all your heart. It is only in response to the love we have for God that we can truly accomplish the second: love our neighbor as ourselves.

The very next story Luke recorded was that of Martha steaming in the kitchen.

Are readers meant to connect them? There are good reasons to assume so. The story of the good Samaritan starts out with the phrase "a certain man." Martha is similarly identified: "a certain woman."[18] Furthermore, Luke made a point by comparing a man and a woman with side-by-side accounts throughout his gospel. For instance, at Christ's birth, Luke contrasted male and female reactions to the angel's announcement: Zacharias's versus Mary's.[19] The sinful woman who lovingly anointed Jesus with oil was portrayed against the cynical Simon the Pharisee.[20] A poor widow's selfless giving was set side by side with rich men's perfunctory offerings.[21]

Here Luke paired the good Samaritan with Martha of Bethany. Both protagonists performed the service of hospitality. One was serving out of love. The other was not.

Jesus told Martha, "Only one thing is necessary." What is the one thing? It all goes back to the commands the lawyer quoted: you shall love the Lord your God with all your heart . . . and your neighbor as yourself. The two stories that follow his recitation explain the commands in reverse order. The good Samaritan fleshes out the second: loving one's neighbor. Martha's story embodies the need for the first: begin by loving God.

Service, when done as an end unto itself, can quickly become burdensome. A lasting sense of satisfaction can come only from our relationship with God. Too often, we skip over that important component and jump right into doing things for him. But far more than he wants our accomplishments, God wants our hearts.

Mary chose the good part. Her being was centered on the Lord, his teaching, his presence. Everything that needed doing paled in comparison. Nothing aced the presence of the man reclining in her dining room. So she faced almost certain censure by abandoning her duties and ignoring social mores to drop down to sit at the feet of the one she loved.

So what was Jesus offering to Martha? It was a gentle invitation for Martha to embrace him with all of her heart as her sister had. The ensuing relationship would change everything. It would furnish the perspective and meaning that would make Martha's service a joy rather than a burden. Knowing Christ more intimately would give her peace.

For Today's Woman

Are you a Martha? Does your attitude suffer at times as you serve because you do not sense appreciation or fail to receive recognition for what you do?

Service in itself is not bad. It's a God-given mandate, an essential part of living our lives for Christ. But if we neglect the good part, loving him with all of our hearts, souls, minds, and strength, our service will not be joyful or fulfilling. It will eventually become a burden. Rather than fill us with contentment and satisfaction, service will suck the life out of us.

How can we know whether we have Martha's problem? We can detect several helpful indications from her story that can warn us when we, too, need a perspective adjustment. The first red flag was Martha's critical spirit toward her sister, evidenced by harsh judgment of her sister's actions. The presence of a critical spirit often shows itself in a warped satisfaction in finding fault with others who serve. We lose sight of the fact that we are all on the same team, serving the same Lord! When we start thinking it's us against them, something is terribly wrong.

The second red flag was the recurring use of the word *me*. Remember what Martha said. "Lord, do you not care that my sister has left *me* to do all the serving by *myself*? Then tell her to help *me*," she commanded. When our agenda becomes self-focused, warning bells should begin to ring. It shouldn't be about us at all.

The third flag, and this one can often remain camou-flaged, is feeling a need to control things. Martha felt justified in ordering people around to accomplish her agenda. She tried to force Mary to return to the kitchen. She even attempted to tell Jesus what to do! Martha was all about taking charge.

My father used to say I was bossy. My teachers tactfully called it leadership potential. But however you label it, I am very comfortable telling everyone what to do! This can be a good thing if it is a gift exercised in submission to the Holy Spirit. But needing to always take charge can be a red flag. Feeling a need to control can come from a self-serving agenda. Oh, we can disguise the motivation, hiding behind altruistic motives. Believe me, I speak from experience.

Years ago I was involved as a vocalist on our church worship team. We had a wonderfully talented group, and leading worship together on Sundays was a thrill. We had some golden years when the team functioned well as a unit, and we had a blast working together. But then everything changed. Our leader left, and the guy who took over was completely different in his leadership style and taste in music. I imme-diately perceived him as a threat to the team's effectiveness in ministry and felt personally responsible to keep him in line. Every change he tried to implement, I resisted. I didn't like the new music he introduced. I didn't like the way he ran rehearsals. I didn't like his new rules and regulations.

No one likes change. But I believed I had *spiritual* reasons to dislike it: *I* was working to keep the spiritual integrity of the team intact. After a couple of years of my self-righteous behavior, which resulted in nothing but misery for him and me, things came to a head. We were arguing at a particularly tense team meeting about the use of music stands. Angrily I shot out: "Well, when our previous leader was here, who, by the way, was a *real* musician . . ."

As soon as the words came out of my mouth, the reality of my motivation for the past two years crashed down on me. My hurtful words, spoken in an attempt to control, revealed a glaring absence of love. Suddenly it was crystal clear: it was all about me, what I wanted, what I thought best. So much for being spiritual!

Paul tells us that service without love is meaningless. "If I speak with the tongues of men and of angels, but do not have love, I have become a noisy gong or a clanging cymbal."[22] Exercising our spiritual gifts must come out of our love for God. Otherwise, rather than working together as an orchestra to produce a beautiful harmony of sound, those who serve will only produce toneless, dissonant noise. Love for God is the key to keeping our efforts at service meaningful.

You can't have that kind of foundational love for God without knowing him. A relationship takes time to develop. He has revealed all he wants us to know about him in his Word. He communicates to us through his Holy Spirit in prayer, should we actually take time to listen. He teaches us about himself through godly people in our lives. For him, it is all about the relationship. It should be for us, too, because neglecting the good part will spell disaster for our service.

When we fall in love with the Lord, our cup overflows. He fills us with his love in such abundance that it spills over into the lives of others. We begin to see people through his eyes. He loves them deeply and wants us to love them too. No longer can our work be about us—we now do it for the benefit of others.

Our need for control vanishes. We begin to look for the ways God is moving rather than remaining blindly focused on achieving our own agendas. We understand it is the Lord's work and not up to us to keep everything in line. What a relief! Carrying the responsibility for everything on our shoulders is a heavy burden. Change no longer threatens us. Instead, we peacefully sit back and wait to see how God will use the change for his glory. Rather than react in anger, we respond in love. And we save ourselves a boatload of misery in the end.

Not long ago, our pastor moved to a new church across the country. Initially I was upset. What would happen to our little church without him to lead? My husband, who headed the search committee, reassured me with his confidence in God. "This is God's church, God's work," he reminded me. "He'll bring the right person along at the right time. We just need to continue to love him and serve faithfully. God will direct and guide." And that was exactly what God did. He brought the right man into the position. He even caused encouraging church growth in the year and a half we moved forward with no pastor at the helm!

There is no need to control if you have confidence in the

One who holds all things together. When you know and love God, you can relax in the goodness and power that are his.

Martha's conversation with Jesus in Luke ended with his directive to seek out the good part. But that was not the end of her story. John recorded another, later conversation and a second meal at her home.[23] Mary and Martha's brother, Lazarus, was deathly ill. She and Mary sent a desperate plea for Jesus to come. Jesus deeply loved Martha, Mary, and Lazarus. But he did the opposite of what they asked. He remained where he was for two more days.

Lazarus died.

It was all a part of God's plan. Jesus would raise Lazarus from the dead, supplying undeniable confirmation in Judea that he was God in the flesh, the Messiah come to free his people. In witnessing that miracle, the Pharisees would understand he was a force to be reckoned with, an undeniable threat to their power as religious leaders of Israel. It would light a fire under them to destroy him before they lost control completely, setting the wheels in motion for the crucifixion that Jesus had planned on from the beginning.

Martha didn't know any of this. All she knew was that her beloved brother was lying cold and lifeless in the grave. When Jesus finally showed up, Martha rushed out to greet him. Her first words reflected her deep sorrow: "Lord, if You had been here, my brother would not have died." Was Martha once again expressing displeasure in Christ's way of doing things? We might be tempted to think so until we read her next statement: "Even now I know that whatever You ask of God, God will give You." Martha was not casting aspersions on Jesus at all. She was expressing her firm belief in his power and wisdom, trusting in his unrelenting obedience to the will of the Father.

A few sentences later, Martha demonstrated the depth of her understanding with a stunning statement of faith. What she revealed fully encompasses the very nature of Jesus and was not uttered by any other person in the Gospels aside from Peter.[24] "I have believed that You are the Christ, the Son of God, even He who comes into the world," she said.

John later used the same words to state the reason for his gospel: "These have been written so that you may believe that Jesus is the Christ, the Son of God; and that believing you may have life in His name."[25] Martha's statement about Jesus at Lazarus's tomb is the gospel in a nutshell, clear, succinct, and insightful. She understood what most of his disciples did not until after his resurrection.

From where did that brilliant insight come? In the conversation, Jesus told Martha he was the resurrection and the life. Did she believe that? Martha assured him: "Yes, Lord; I have believed." The verb tense is perfect indicative: it indicates a previously completed action that affects the speaker's present. In other words, Martha believed a while ago. She was able to state what she did because of that belief.

I think we can assume Martha did exactly what Jesus advised the night of her first big dinner party. She made it her business to get to know him. What she learned enabled her to trust him even when his chosen absence caused her beloved brother's demise. She knew his character, and she knew who he was. So in spite of the devastating circumstances, she trusted him.

Further evidence of Martha's deeper relationship with Jesus comes in the very next chapter of John. Jesus once again was dining at Martha's home. Martha once again was working in the kitchen. For a second time, Mary went AWOL, this time to anoint Jesus with perfume and wipe his feet with her hair. But this time we see no unhappiness expressed by Martha as she served her Lord. She quietly went about her responsibilities without comment on her sister's repeated desertion.

Martha found her center, her focus, her reason for serving. She knew him, she loved him, and she trusted in his wisdom and character. No longer was she driven to control the situation or compare herself with others. It was no longer about her at all, but about the one she was serving. Gone were the distractions of anxiety and anger. Martha could serve in peace, even while sweating in the heat of the kitchen. Her service was for Jesus alone.

Like Martha, we must recognize that our antidote for anxiety and trouble lies in drawing close to the Savior. As we learn from him and learn to trust in who he is, our love for him will grow. Service will be merely an outflow of the relationship. We will be free to work without anger because we are not doing it for recognition or any other self-serving motive. We serve freely because we understand how freely we are loved. When our focus is where it should be, we will have only joy in service.

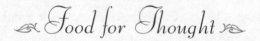

Food for Thought

1. Do you relate more to Martha or Mary? Why?
2. Can you think of a time when the red flags that Martha exhibited have been true of you as well? Think through what your

motivations were at the time. Can you identify ways in which your agenda was self-focused?

3. Read Ephesians 3:14–19. Why do you think Paul prayed that for the Ephesians? How is it important to the unity in service he urged for his readers? How would it equip them to serve and effectively build the body of Christ?

4. What specific things can you do to move yourself deeper into your relationship with God? Keep your ideas practical, noting specific action. Plan small, obtainable goals. Remember, perseverance is more important than perfection.

≈ *Journaling* ≈

How much does your love for God characterize your service? Do you burn out easily? Take offense at a lack of recognition? Find in yourself a tendency to judge others? Feel a need to control? These are all symptoms of a bigger issue.

Take an honest look at the emotions that your efforts at service tend to bring out in you. List the ways in which you struggle. Then try to see the situation with God's perspective. What is his ultimate goal? Is it seeing the work accomplished, or the transformation he desires to bring about in each person involved? Write a letter from God to yourself. What does he want you to remember as you serve him? How does he want you to reflect his love for you in your actions toward others?

chapter seven

He needed to go through Samaria.

So He came to a city of Samaria which is called Sychar, near the plot of ground that Jacob gave to his son Joseph. Now Jacob's well was there. Jesus therefore, being wearied from His journey, sat thus by the well. It was about the sixth hour.

A woman of Samaria came to draw water. Jesus said to her, "Give Me a drink." For His disciples had gone away into the city to buy food.

Then the woman of Samaria said to Him, "How is it that You, being a Jew, ask a drink from me, a Samaritan woman?" For Jews have no dealings with Samaritans.

Jesus answered and said to her, "If you knew the gift of God, and who it is who says to you, 'Give Me a drink,' you would have asked Him, and He would have given you living water."

The woman said to Him, "Sir, You have nothing to draw with, and the well is deep. Where then do You get that living water? Are You greater than our father Jacob, who gave us the well, and drank from it himself, as well as his sons and his livestock?"

Jesus answered and said to her, "Whoever drinks of this water will thirst again, but whoever drinks of the water that I shall give him will never thirst. But the water that I shall give him will become in him a fountain of water springing up into everlasting life."

The woman said to Him, "Sir, give me this water, that I may not thirst, nor come here to draw."

Jesus said to her, "Go, call your husband, and come here."

The woman answered and said, "I have no husband."

Jesus said to her, "You have well said, 'I have no husband,' for you have had five husbands, and the one whom you now have is not your husband; in that you spoke truly."

The woman said to Him, "Sir, I perceive that You are a prophet. Our fathers worshiped on this mountain, and you Jews say that in Jerusalem is the place where one ought to worship."

Jesus said to her, "Woman, believe Me, the hour is coming when you will neither on this mountain, nor in Jerusalem, worship the Father. You worship what you do not know; we know what we worship, for salvation is of the Jews. But the hour is coming, and now is, when the true worshipers will worship the Father in spirit and truth; for the Father is seeking such to worship Him. God is Spirit, and those who worship Him must worship in spirit and truth."

The woman said to Him, "I know that Messiah is coming" (who is called Christ). "When He comes, He will tell us all things."

Jesus said to her, "I who speak to you am He."

And at this point His disciples came, and they marveled that He talked with a woman; yet no one said, "What do You seek?" or, "Why are You talking with her?"

The woman then left her waterpot, went her way into the city, and said to the men, "Come, see a Man who told me all things that I ever did. Could this be the Christ?" Then they went out of the city and came to Him.

—JOHN 4:4–30 NKJV

Thirsty for More than Water

JESUS AND THE SAMARITAN WOMAN

While on a routine chore to collect water at the town well, a Samaritan woman meets Jesus. Their conversation takes many puzzling twists and turns, quickly transitioning from living water to her marital history to the appropriate place to worship God. How did the differences between Samaritan and Jew necessitate what was discussed between them? What ultimately was said that enabled her to understand Jesus was not only the Jewish Messiah, but her Messiah as well?

t was a hot, dry, dusty afternoon. While most of the village women walked to the well together in the cool of the morning or evening, this woman walked the path alone in the heat of the day. She wasn't the kind of woman with whom decent women associated. Tired of their condemning stares and pointed silence, she chose to draw her water in the relative safety the stifling heat provided.

The sun blazed down on her head as she approached her destination. She noticed a stranger sitting on the stone wall at the edge of the well. Travelers often stopped at Jacob's Well for refreshment; it was a well-known landmark. Yet this stranger was unusual to the outskirts of Sychar in the heart of Samaria. By the blue trim on the bottom of his robe, she could see right away that he was a Jew.

There was no love lost between her people, the Samaritans, and the Jews. Their particular animosity began hundreds of years ago. Some Jews would cross the Jordan on their trip between Galilee and Judea and traverse gentile territory rather than step foot on Samaritan soil. So it was a surprise to find this Jew lingering at the low stone wall outside Sychar.

Keeping her gaze trained on the ground, she carefully avoided eye contact with him and moved to draw water from the deep well. To her surprise, the man spoke to her. "Give me a drink?" he gently requested.

A Jew, speaking to a Samaritan? A Samaritan woman, no less? "You are asking me, a Samaritan woman, to give you a drink?" she blurted out. Any other Jew would rather die of thirst than speak to a Samaritan woman!

She was about to learn this was no ordinary Jew. He answered, "If you knew the gift of God, and who it is who says to you, 'Give me a drink,' *you* would be asking *me* for a drink. And I would give you living water." Her curiosity was piqued. How could he sit there offering water, when he obviously didn't have a jar to lower into the well?

"You have nothing to draw with, and the well is deep," she reminded him. "So how are you going to get this water? You are not greater than our father Jacob, are you, who gave us the well, and drank of it himself and his sons and his cattle?" Even Jacob, who dug the well, could not get water from it without a utensil.

He appeared unfazed by her challenge and stated, "Everyone who drinks of the water that I will give him shall never thirst; but the water that I will give him will become in him a well of water springing up to eternal life."

What was he talking about? Surely not ordinary water from a well! Was he offering some magical elixir that would keep her from ever being thirsty again? The conversation had taken a strange turn, but she decided to play along.

She told him, "Sir, give me this water, so I will not be thirsty, nor have to come all the way here to draw." She waited to see what he would say next.

His answer was not what she expected. "Go," he said. "Call your husband and come here."

She understood it was natural for him to assume that she was a married woman. After all, she was no longer a young girl, and one look at her face would have revealed an obviously hard-lived existence. Of course, he could have no idea of her complicated marital history. She kept her response simple but honest. "I have no husband," she told him.

Even though her gaze remained stubbornly downward, she could feel his eyes boring into her. What he said next nearly knocked the breath out of her: "What you have just said is quite true. The fact is, you have had five husbands, and the man you now have is not your husband."

Her jaw dropped. She had never seen this man before in her life, and he knew of her whole sorry past? Who *was* this man? Heart thumping, she dared to lift her gaze to meet his, wholly expecting condemnation and censure. Instead, his eyes reflected a gentle understanding. Even though he somehow knew the worst, his purpose in revealing it did not seem to be reproachful. Instead, he seemed to be peering into her very soul, seeing straight to the aching neediness in her heart.

For most of her adult life, men had treated her as merely a possession. Her marital history was a sad record of relationships gone bad. Over time she had learned to use what feminine charms she possessed to attract a new provider when necessary. It was not easy for a woman to live without the protection of a man. But she had a roof over her head and food in her bowl. She had done what it took to survive.

Although much of her youthful beauty was now gone, men were still attracted to her. Because of her past, they thought of her as a loose woman. She would often see them leering at her in the marketplace, their lustful thoughts made obvious by the intense light in their eyes. She hated this.

Yet this Jew did not look at her in the same way as the men in her village. There was no judgment in his gaze, nor did he make any sexual innuendos with his words or expressions.

In that moment, she knew instinctively that he was no ordinary man. "Sir," she said, the light slowly dawning, "I perceive that you are a prophet."

But if he was a Jewish prophet, his interest in her was surely misplaced. The Jews and Samaritans were two different peoples with histories and religions poles apart. If he was a prophet, then he was obviously a prophet sent to the Jews. Why was he here in this place, reaching out to her?

"Our fathers worshipped on this mountain," she reminded him, gesturing to Mount Gerazim, which lay directly behind them, "and you people say that Jerusalem is the place where men ought to worship." Surely he must know that a Jewish prophet should have no interest in a Samaritan's problems.

He gestured dismissively, as if the great gulf between Jew and Samaritan were of no consequence. "Woman, believe me," he stated. "An hour is coming when neither in this mountain nor in Jerusalem will you worship the Father. True worshippers will worship the Father in spirit and in truth, for such people the Father seeks to be his worshippers. God is Spirit, and those who worship him must worship in spirit and truth."

She had only a limited understanding of religion, since she'd never received a formal education. She did know that a great prophet, the Messiah, had been promised by Moses, one who would be a teacher with even greater authority than Moses himself. Could this actually be him? He certainly had a knowledge of her that could not be explained in human terms. "I know that the Messiah is coming. When he comes, he will declare all things to us," she told him.

He looked her straight in the eye, a half-smile on his lips. "I am he," he said.

The power of that simple acknowledgment nearly bowled her over. She believed him. He knew her past. He knew the future. He spoke with purposeful authority. She felt certain he was as he claimed.

There was so much more she wanted to ask him, so much she wanted to say. But at that moment, a large group of men came walking from the direction of town over to where they stood. As they exchanged greetings with Jesus, they looked at her with great curiosity. They seemed to barely restrain themselves from demanding the obvious: Why are you speaking with a Samaritan woman?

Uncomfortable with their staring, struck with a sense of urgency, she turned toward town. She needed to get the word out to her people before he left the area. Forgetting her water pot in her haste, she hurried into the city to inform the men at the city gates of her discovery.

Arriving at the gate, she begged them, "Come, there is a man at the well who was able to tell me all the things that I have done. I think he is the Christ!" Hearing the urgency in her words and the conviction in her voice, the men hurried back to the well with her to see the man for themselves.

Digging Deeper

Why was there such animosity between the Jews and the Samaritans?

The hostility between these two people groups was centuries old. But it hadn't always been that way. At one time, the twelve tribes of Israel were united under one God and one king. The people had originally covenanted with God to worship only him. But eventually the sensual religion of the surrounding people groups turned the heads of the Israelites. Slowly but surely, idol worship became commonplace in Israel.

This grave sin extended to the highest office of the land. Solomon, one of the greatest Israelite kings who ever ruled, married foreign wives and began to worship their strange gods. God announced his judgment, for this would fall on the coming generation: a civil war would tear the kingdom in two, never to be reunited under self-rule again.

In 930 BC, God made good on his threat. Rebelling against Solomon's son, the ten tribes of the north united to become the northern kingdom of Israel. The remaining two tribes became the kingdom of Judah.

Of the two kingdoms, Israel was by far the more corrupt. A wicked line of kings openly worshipped false gods and led the people into severe moral decline. After two hundred some years, the patience of God had come to an end. The Lord sent the Assyrian army in 722 BC to put an end to the Northern Kingdom.

Many were carried off by their captors. The Assyrians had a policy of resettling a newly conquered land with conquered peoples from other nations. They repopulated the former Northern Kingdom with foreigners. The Jews who remained in the land intermarried with their new neighbors. This mixed racial group became known by the region in which they lived: Samaria.

One hundred thirty-six years after the fall of the Northern Kingdom, the southern kingdom of Judah also suffered judgment for its decline into idol worship. In 586 BC, Judah fell to the Babylonian Empire. Many Jews were taken away to live in the region of Babylon. Decades later, a group of those exiled Jews was allowed to return. They arrived to find the city of Jerusalem not much more than a pile of rubble. Led by Nehemiah and Ezra, they purposed to rebuild the wall around the city and the temple.

The Samaritans, who had continued to live in the land during their absence, came and offered assistance as construction began. They were not welcome, however. In the eyes of the Jews, who had remained racially and religiously pure even during the Exile, the Samaritans were worse than Gentiles. They had lost their right to be called Jews and had no right to share in the honor of rebuilding the temple. The insulted Samaritans turned on their neighbors and even hired thugs to frustrate the Jews in the project. The hatred between the Samaritans and the Jews intensified.

Centuries later, when the Romans conquered the land, they united the remains of the former two kingdoms into an uneasy union. The land was sectioned into provinces. On the west side of the Jordan, Galilee was in the north, Samaria directly below it, and Judea the southernmost province.

The Jews of Judea and Galilee considered the Samaritans half-breeds and an unclean people. Fear of contamination drove some to sidestep Samaritan land altogether should a journey become necessary between Judea and Galilee. Rejecting the most direct route, they crossed the river and traveled parallel to Samaria, lengthening a three-day journey into six. That was not necessarily a routine choice, according to the ancient historian Josephus.[1] But the fact that it was done at all shows the strong animosity continuing to the time of Jesus.

Samaritan women were especially repugnant to a male Jew. Later that century, their distaste would be reflected in a rabbinic writing that declared Samaritan women menstruants from their cradle, perpetually in a state of ceremonial uncleanliness.[2] This expressed sentiment certainly explains why the Samaritan woman was so amazed that Jesus would strike up a conversation with her. It truly was an unusual occurrence.

*How did Samaritans' religion differ from that of their
Jewish neighbors?*

By the time Jesus sat on the well wall conversing with the
Samaritan woman, Samaritan polytheism had long disappeared. The Samaritans then worshipped the God of the Bible
alone.[3] However, their version of religion had striking differences from traditional Judaism.

After being rejected from participating in the rebuilding
of Jerusalem, the Samaritans built a temple of their own on
the plateau-like summit of Mount Gerazim.[4] They believed
this mountain to be a holy spot, God's chosen place of spiritual blessing. They adjusted their version of history to support
their choice of temple location. Samaritans believed that
Mount Gerazim was where Abraham attempted to sacrifice
his son Isaac and where Melchizedek appeared to Abraham.[5]
Gerazim was where they believed Moses commanded the
people to erect an altar and sacrifice to God upon their
arrival in the promised land.[6] They also (this time accurately)
believed Gerazim was where half the tribes of Israel shouted
about the blessings of God to those on the opposite hillside of
Mount Ebal after crossing the Jordan.[7] The Samaritan temple
was destroyed by the Jews during the Maccabean days in 129
BC.[8] But the site continued to be of religious importance to
the Samaritans well beyond Jesus' day.

The town of Sychar, where the Samaritan woman lived,
was located on the slope of Mount Ebal and overlooked
Mount Gerazim. The Samaritan woman had been brought up
to regard Mount Gerazim as holy ground and the center for
worship. But she also knew the Jews just as firmly believed
Jerusalem to be the most sacred of places.

Another big difference between Samaritan and Jewish beliefs was in the portions of Scripture deemed authoritative. The Samaritans did not recognize the majority of the Old Testament, which had been canonized by religious leaders in Judea. According to the Samaritans, the Pentateuch alone (the first five books of the Old Testament) was the inspired Word of God. The vast majority of messianic prophecies are contained in the Psalms and the Prophets. Therefore the Samaritan understanding about him was severely limited.

What was Jesus offering the Samaritan woman?

Jesus said to her: "If you knew the gift of God, and who it is who says to you, 'Give Me a drink,' you would have asked Him, and He would have given you living water." What would the phrase "living water" have meant to someone in first-century Samaria?

Water could be collected from two kinds of sources. One could draw from a pool of standing water, like a cistern or a pond. But the preferred source would be running water, like from a stream or bubbling spring, where the water would be naturally fresh and clean. This kind of water was referred to as "living water" in Jesus' day.

Although the Samaritan woman didn't pick up on it right away, Jesus was using living water as a metaphor to picture the gift he was offering to all who would believe. What was this gift? We get insight into what it was from other passages in John's gospel.

John the Baptist informed his followers, "He who sent me to baptize in water said to me, 'He upon whom you see the Spirit descending and remaining upon Him, this is the One who baptizes in the Holy Spirit.'"[9] Jesus was coming to enact a whole new kind of baptism: while John baptized with physical water, Jesus would baptize believers with living water, the Holy Spirit, who would usher in new and eternal life. Jesus later expounded on this idea: "He who believes in Me . . . 'From his innermost being will flow rivers of living water.'"[10] John explained, "This he spoke of the Spirit, whom those who believed in Him were to receive."[11]

Why did Jesus suddenly bring up the woman's past?

Now he had her interest. She took the bait. "Sir, give me this water," she told him, "so I will not be thirsty or have to come all the way here to draw."

What Jesus revealed in the next segment of conversation seemed to come out of nowhere, catching both the woman and the reader by surprise. He bluntly brought up her five failed marriages and her current immoral living situation. Why did he do that?

His revelation would help her understand not only what he was offering but also how desperately she needed what he wanted to give. He let her know he had seen it all—the good, the bad, and the ugly in her life.

How ugly was it? Commentators through the years have judged the Samaritan woman harshly based on the number of marriages she had as well as the fact she was currently living in sin on the day she met Jesus. They are quick to attribute her failed marriages to some inherent moral failure on her part. That may or may not be the case.

Could she have been just plain unlucky?[12] In the first century, the average life expectancy for those who lived past the age of ten was thirty-eight to fifty years old. Women were frequently widowed and remarried. However, in the ancient texts available to us today, while it was not uncommon to lose two spouses in a lifetime, there is not one other example of a woman widowed and remarried five times.[13]

Divorce initiated by a wife is a rare occurrence in ancient records. Yet the law of Moses allowed a man to divorce his wife should she be found in some "indecency."[14] It is likely the woman had been abandoned by some of her previous husbands. Was this a gross mistreatment or a result of her marital unfaithfulness? We can't know.

The fact that she was living without a marital agreement at the time she met Jesus indicated darker moral issues in her character. Author Lynn Cohick suggests she may have been living as a concubine, possibly in a relationship with a Roman citizen who could not marry beneath his social rank.[15] Alternatively she could have been taken as a second wife to a man already married. Polygamous relationships were not uncommon in first-century Palestine.

Whatever her circumstances, victim or sinner or maybe a combination of both, her long list of failures must have played a factor in how her community viewed her and ultimately in how she viewed herself.

Jesus was inviting her to an intimate relationship with God. There cannot be intimacy without full knowledge. Before such a relationship could be established, she must know that he knew the worst and that he wanted her anyway. She had to know that the grace he offered would cover it all. It would wash away every bit of her shame. There would be no dark secrets left to fester.

We don't deal with cancer by slapping on a Band-Aid. It would continue to eat away at the healthy cells until it took over and killed the body. Rather, the surgeon skillfully exposes and removes the sick, corrupted cells. Only then can true healing begin.

So for the Samaritan woman, Jesus left no stone unturned. The exposure was purposed to bring a curative effect to her deepest, most secret parts. It would only serve to heal. As Jesus told Nicodemus in John's previous chapter, "God did not send his Son into the world to condemn the world, but to save the world through him."[16]

So as shaming as it might have been for her to hear the words said aloud, it was also freeing to have everything out in the open. There were no deep secrets left to guard from discovery. He already knew it all and loved her regardless.

Why did she start talking about the differences between Samaritan and Jewish worship?

In yet another quick turn in the conversation, the woman seemed to suddenly shift the subject. Was she doing so out of embarrassment after hearing about her past? Or was she somehow moving forward on the same path Jesus started them on to begin with?

The Samaritan woman knew a bit about the promised Messiah. In Deuteronomy the Lord informed Moses: "I will raise up a prophet from among their countrymen like you, and I will put My words in his mouth, and he shall speak to them all that I command him."[17] Like all Samaritans, she looked for a prophet greater than Moses who would come and explain all spiritual matters to those whom he would lead.

Jesus had just demonstrated an ability to know things an ordinary man could not have known. No one could have done this unless empowered by God. Obviously this man was a prophet. Maybe *the* Prophet.

But he was a *Jewish* prophet. That big problem must somehow be overcome before she could truly accept the gift he offered. She was Samaritan, after all, not Jewish. Her people still worshipped at Mount Gerazim. The religious practices with which she was raised were in conflict with what Jews practiced in Galilee and Judea. She was not changing the subject! She was bringing up what she saw as an enormous obstacle to accepting his living water.

Jesus responded in a way that must have surprised her once again. He did not pick sides, arguing whether one set of practices was more valid than the other, for with his coming, such things would cease to be an issue. Everything was about to change—and change radically.

"An hour is coming, and now is, when the true worshippers will worship the Father in spirit and truth," he informed her. "For the Father seeks such people to be his worshippers." No longer would the place matter where worship was offered. For Jews, Gentiles, or Samaritans, a day was coming when a person would not be identified by his or her external place of worship. The mark would be internal: one's relationship with the Son of God.

"I am the way and the truth and the life," Jesus would later inform his disciples. "No one comes to the Father except through me."[18] God stood outside the culture that had been the framework of the woman's understanding of him. He was beckoning her to join him, calling her to believe in his Son. He was inviting her to give him her heart.

She needed to be sure she understood. "I know that Messiah is coming (he who is called Christ). When that one comes, he will declare all things to us," she told him. It mattered who he was. She had to be very sure.

"I am he," he reassured her. The original Greek reads *ego eimi*. I AM. It was the same way God identified himself to Moses at the burning bush: "Thus you shall say to the sons of Israel, 'I AM has sent me to you.'"[19] These simple words of Jesus were an identification with the deity of God. There was great power in those three syllables. On the night of his arrest, the soldiers told Jesus they were seeking to arrest Jesus the Nazarene. "I am He," he simply said. The power of that statement overwhelmed the fierce Roman cohort and temple officers and literally threw them to the ground.[20]

It was all the Samaritan woman needed to hear. He was the Messiah. He had proved it with his inexplicable knowledge of her dismal life. He had offered her new life, living water. She believed.

Why did Jesus so easily admit he was the Messiah to her when so many other times in the Gospels he told people to keep quiet about his identity?

A read through the Gospels reveals Jesus' admission to the woman at the well to be an exception to his normal reluctance to identify himself as the Messiah. Why, then, did he feel free to identify himself to this woman?

Again, the differences in the expectations of the Samaritans versus the Jews regarding the coming Messiah are key to understanding this. The Samaritans were not looking for a Messiah who would bring political freedom from Roman oppression.

Rather, they anticipated a prophet who would primarily be a spiritual teacher. Revealing his identity would not spur the Samaritans to revolt as it might the people in Judea or Galilee, where the people yearned for a Messiah to lead them against their Roman oppressors. So Jesus could divulge the truth without fear of people getting sidetracked with aspirations of political freedom.

Jesus was willing to proclaim his identity to Gentiles as well. In Galilee or Judea, he frequently warned those he healed not to tell others, but he told the demoniac in Gerasa (located in gentile territory) to report to the town what had been done for him. With Gentiles there was no danger that word would spread through the Jewish grapevine. So Jesus used his contact with them to plant seeds that would be harvested by the apostles after the resurrection.[21]

For Today's Woman

The story of the Samaritan woman has a scriptural counterpart in the Old Testament. In Genesis, we meet Hagar, a woman whose nationality would similarly make her an unlikely candidate for God's personal attentions.[22]

As an Egyptian slave, Hagar led a life that was far from ideal. Taken from her family and home country and forced into slavery, she existed only to benefit others. The lack of concern afforded to her by her owners was apparent in the way they addressed her, referring to her only as "my servant," never once actually calling her by name. She had no say even over her own body—to her owners, she was just one more possession.

God had promised Hagar's master, Abram, a son, then waited twenty-five years to deliver on that promise. While they waited, Abram's wife, Sarai, grew impatient and decided to take action. She urged her husband to take Hagar as his wife and impregnate her as a surrogate. It worked.

Not surprisingly, friction began almost immediately between the two women, as Sarai, long burdened with her barrenness, struggled with Hagar's new, elevated status of carrying the heir and her resulting disdain for Sarai. Hagar didn't stand a chance. Holding all the power, Sarai began to mistreat Hagar (with the law's and Abram's blessing). Things got so bad that Hagar finally fled, choosing the perils of a desert journey (while pregnant, no less!) rather than face continued abuse.

She headed south, back toward her homeland, into the harsh desert. She was alone, destitute, and desperate. It was there, by a spring, that the angel of the Lord sought her out. "Hagar, servant of Sarai, where have you come from, and where are you going?" he asked. She might have been nameless to her masters, but God knew her name.

After Hagar explained her need to run, the angel of the Lord told her, "Go back to your mistress and submit to her." Then, to reassure her that God had good things in mind for her, he added, "I will so increase your descendants that they will be too numerous to count." He followed this statement by prophesying about her unborn child, giving details of what would be his life.

Many scholars believe encounters with the angel of the Lord are actually appearances of the preincarnate Christ. There are many Old Testament examples: Moses at the burning bush, Balaam and his donkey, and Gideon, just to name a few.[23] The

angel of the Lord approached the person, who at the beginning of the conversation was usually clueless about the speaker's
identity. He used pronouns like *me* and *I* as he delivered God's
words, making it sound as if God himself was speaking, not
just a messenger. Finally, either as the conversation wore on or
as it came to an end, the person realized that he or she had "seen
the Lord." The New Testament never confirms that the angel
of the Lord is actually God, but many scholars have reached the
conclusion it could only be him—and as he was in man form,
that it must be the preincarnate Christ.

This interesting possibility makes Hagar's experience with
the angel of the Lord that much more analogous to that of the
Samaritan woman. Two women, alone and mistreated, met
Jesus at a well. Both got a new understanding of who he really
was as they conversed with him. Both came away understanding a powerful truth: the God they knew only in principle was
aware of their most personal details.

Neither was a chance meeting. Each woman was specifically sought out. The angel of the Lord followed Hagar into
the wilderness. Jesus did not need to travel through Samaria;
most Jews avoided that route as a matter of habit, as I have
noted. He went to Sychar in obedience to the Spirit's leading.
He had a divine appointment with a woman whose thirst only
he could quench.

Before their encounters, both women knew a thing or two
about God. Hagar had lived her adult life in the household
of Abram, a man who worshipped the true, living God. He
had experienced personal conversations with God and staked
his life on his promises. A covenant had been established. No
doubt this agreement affected the entire camp, where no idols

would have been allowed and immorality would have been discouraged. So Hagar knew plenty about God and probably could have instructed a newcomer on the subject. She knew *about* God. But she didn't *know* him.

The Samaritan woman's questions revealed a working knowledge of the basics. She knew who God was and about his plan to send the Messiah. She knew of the Pentateuch, the Law, and the worship that God desired. She most likely participated on some level in the culture of her people's religion. But God wanted her knowledge of him to transcend the culture, for what she knew in her head hadn't quite made it into her heart.

A friend of mine was married to a pastor. As they worked side by side in ministry, she relied more and more on her husband in her spiritual walk. Eventually her understanding of God became largely based on her husband's knowledge and experience, rather than her personal interaction with him. When her husband died, she found herself armed for life as a widow with not much more than useless pat answers and platitudes. What had become a shallow relationship with God was totally inadequate. It was high time to seek God on an intimate level for herself.

You really can't get to know God through someone else's experience.

Another friend of mine was an important part of a Christian organization. She was well versed in its theology and fit right into the culture. People admired her wisdom and sought out her counsel. But when she left her job behind, the bottom fell out of her spiritual walk. In the end, she realized her spirituality had been all about being part of a group, fitting in with the culture. When that disappeared, she found her relationship with God to be only skin-deep.

Being part of a Christian organization doesn't give you a relationship with God any more than touring the White House makes you the president.

God doesn't want a vicarious relationship with us, established through the experiences and theology of others. He wants *us*. He wants our hearts. He wanted the same for Hagar and the Samaritan woman. Their vicarious experience would not suffice. So he purposefully encountered them, face-to-face. He showed them just how well he knew them, and in doing so he urged them to get to know him with the same kind of passion. Practicing religion or having the ability to parrot someone else's theology just isn't enough. It has to be personal.

So he pursues us, just as determinedly as he did the Samaritan woman and Hagar. He reveals just how well he knows us, and he invites us to know and love him with the same passion he has invested in us.

Both Hagar and the Samaritan woman were swept off their feet by God's advances. Hagar responded in awe and gave God a name: *El Roi*, the God who Sees.[24] Then she obeyed his instruction and headed back to Abram's camp. The Samaritan woman responded in similar fashion. Dropping her water jar in her haste, she dashed off to tell the town of the man by the well. But notice the first words that came from her lips—she didn't talk about theology or even the living water of which she and Jesus spoke. What got top billing? His knowledge of the personal details in her life: "Come, see a man who told me everything I ever did."

For both women, God's knowledge of their personal details was the catalyst and basis for an intimate relationship with him.

An intimate relationship was what he had in mind for an Egyptian slave and a half-breed Samaritan. And it's what he has in mind for us. Like the Samaritan woman, we live with a thirst that only he can satisfy. He invites us to know him one-on-one, away from the noise of religion and Christian culture. He has revealed himself with clarity and detail in his Word. He's the God who Sees. And he wants us to see him right back.

⤖ Food for Thought ⤖

1. Much of the Samaritan woman's religion was wrapped up in her culture. In what ways does the culture of your church define how you think about God? Are there ways we have attached Jesus to a particular culture that may be an impediment to people believing in him? How can we avoid this?

2. Jesus told the woman: "The hour is coming, and now is, when the true worshipers will worship the Father in spirit and truth; for the Father is seeking such to worship Him. God is Spirit, and those who worship Him must worship in spirit and truth." What do you think he meant? How does this help your understanding of the kind of worship that God seeks from us?

3. Jesus offered the Samaritan living water. It was a metaphor, a word picture, of new life in Christ. David used the same image in Psalm 42:1–2:

> *As the deer pants for the water brooks,*
> *So my soul pants for You, O God.*
> *My soul thirsts for God, for the living God.*

What kind of thirst do these pictures portray? Be specific. Remember water is not a nice-to-have thing, but an essential to survival. How does the metaphor of living water help us picture what Christ offers us?

4. How does knowing he is the God who Sees help you be honest with him? How does his intimate knowledge affect your desire for a deeper relationship?

❧ *Journaling* ☙

Think about your recent interactions with God. What did they involve? Prayer? Bible study? Fellowship? Listening to teaching? How *personal* was the time you spent with him? Is your experience with God largely dependent on others?

What can you do to go deeper with him, one-on-one? As with any relationship, growth happens through the investment of time and effort by both parties. He has done everything necessary to make a relationship with him possible. In what ways can you invest yourself in return?

Write a letter to God and express your desire to go deeper with him. He will be faithful to respond, as promised in James 4:8: "Draw near to God and He will draw near to you."

chapter eight

Then the mother of the sons of Zebedee came to Jesus with her sons, bowing down and making a request of Him. And He said to her, "What do you wish?"

She said to Him, "Command that in Your kingdom these two sons of mine may sit one on Your right and one on Your left."

But Jesus answered, "You do not know what you are asking. Are you able to drink the cup that I am about to drink?"

They said to Him, "We are able."

He said to them, "My cup you shall drink; but to sit on My right and on My left, this is not Mine to give, but it is for those for whom it has been prepared by My Father."

And hearing this, the ten became indignant with the two brothers.

But Jesus called them to Himself and said, "You know that the rulers of the Gentiles lord it over them, and their great men exercise authority over them. It is not this way among you, but whoever wishes to become great among you shall be your servant, and whoever wishes to be first among you shall be your slave; just as the Son of Man did not come to be served, but to serve, and to give His life a ransom for many."

—MATTHEW 20:20–28

(THIS STORY IS ALSO RECORDED IN MARK 10:35–45.)

Misguided Mother

JESUS AND SALOME

A proud mother speaks up on behalf of her two sons: Would Jesus put them in a place of authority when he established his kingdom? Where did they get the idea of an imminent empire? What was the "cup" Jesus warned they would share with him? How did these disciples from the inner circle get so far off track from what Jesus had been teaching them all along?

It had been a long, exhausting trip to Judea from Galilee. The night before their arrival, James and John took their mother aside. Jesus had privately informed the twelve disciples earlier that day of their ultimate destination: Jerusalem. It appeared that Jesus was finally going to reveal his true identity to the world. Sitting by the crackling campfire, the three speculated on how life would change once Jesus came into power. The young men confided their hope to their mother of being men of great influence in the messianic kingdom. They anticipated being given great responsibility in view of the fact that they and Peter were known as the inner circle. While they conversed over the flickering light of the fire, James had an idea.

"Mother," he said, "it certainly wouldn't hurt for Jesus to be reminded of our faithful service and loyalty. You have been in support of Jesus from the beginning. He might be open to hearing a suggestion from you. If you get an opportunity, could you suggest that John and I rule by his side? It would sound better coming from you than from us."

Salome hesitated. Her boys were not short on nerve. That was for sure. Jesus had aptly nicknamed them Sons of Thunder. James's suggestion seemed audacious. She knew that Jesus encouraged personal, honest communication with all of those who followed him, the women included. Still, she was not used to it, this treatment as an equal. It was so contrary to what she had known in her previous life. Could she dare approach him with such a bold request?

She loved her boys and was proud of the men they had become. Surely Jesus had seen their potential for leadership and was grooming them to take on the responsibility they desired. "I'll do what I can, should the opportunity arise," she acquiesced.

The next morning they broke camp and began the final phase of the journey into Jerusalem. After several hours of walking, the group stopped to rest. Most reclined quietly on the soft grass in the shade of trees, sleepily enjoying the sound of gurgling water from a nearby brook. Salome saw her chance. She moved close to Jesus, who lay gazing at the blue sky overhead, and she perched on a large rock beside him.

"Rabbi," she said softly, hoping the nearby disciples who rested with their eyes closed were truly asleep, "I have something to ask you."

Jesus shifted his gaze and smiled warmly. "What do you wish?" he asked.

"I know you are about to establish your kingdom," she said. "I think that you should give my sons a place of authority. I would like you to establish them with one sitting on your right and one on your left."

Jesus looked past Salome to her sons, who rested just beyond him. He prodded James and John with his foot. Both sat up immediately, eager to hear Jesus' confirmation. But his next words were not what they hoped.

"You do not know what you are asking," he warned them. "Are you able to drink the cup that I am about to drink?"

With their typical confidence, both men quickly affirmed their commitment to Jesus. "Certainly!" they assured him. They had followed him for three years. They had faithfully listened to his teaching and aided him as he ministered to sick and demon-possessed people. They had traveled as his representatives, preaching repentance and his teachings to anyone who would listen. Hadn't they sacrificed everything, homes, family, and livelihood, to follow him? Unquestionably they had proved their loyalty by now. Surely he planned to use his most trusted associates to aid him in his administration.

Jesus' face showed sadness as he considered the two men's reply. Ironically their words were correct, but not their intended meaning. "My cup you shall drink," he said with a sigh. "But to sit on my right and on my left, this is not mine to give, but it is for those for whom it has been prepared by my Father."

Several of the other disciples, having heard at least the last part of the conversation, sat up, indignant that the brothers would make such a request. Why should they be considered above the rest? Hadn't they all been equally committed to the Messiah's future kingdom? Peter especially was miffed—of the inner circle of three, they had neglected to include him. They had gone behind his back! How dare they consider themselves more deserving than he was!

Jesus took the opportunity to once again impress on his disciples the nature of his coming kingdom. If allowed to continue, their misconceptions of future greatness would seriously impact their effectiveness in the work that God planned for them to do. They were viewing God's kingdom through the lens of human understanding. Having a desire for power and authority could not be more opposed to God's way.

"You know that the rulers of other nations lord it over those they rule, taking advantage of every opportunity to use their power for their own benefit," he said. "But that is not how it will work in God's kingdom. Whoever wishes to be the first among you will be your slave. Haven't I already lived this out in front of you? I did not come expecting to be served, but to serve. In fact, I will be giving my very life as a ransom for others!"

John and James looked at their now embarrassed mother in dismay. They had pushed her to speak on their behalf, but their request now seemed shallow and self-serving. The other disciples were eyeing them with mistrust and anger. Once again their boldness had led them into trouble. As they picked up their belongings to get back on the road, each silently promised himself to think before speaking in the future.

$\mathcal{D}$*igging* $\mathcal{D}$*eeper*

Who was Salome?

Salome was the wife of Zebedee, a successful fresh-water fisherman who labored on the Sea of Galilee. They lived in the town of Capernaum, less than twenty miles north of Jesus' hometown of Nazareth. Fishing was a profitable livelihood and a major industry in Galilee. Josephus, an ancient writer at the time of Christ and at one time governor of Galilee, wrote that 330 fishing boats were in business there.[1] Fish was a staple diet item of the Jews, who rarely ate meat more than once a week.[2] Zebedee was affluent enough to hire a crew to work for him.[3] They had at least two adult sons, James and John.

In order to sell their catch, fishermen needed to travel over roads and bridges to their intended buyers. Herod Antipas controlled the harbor and roadways and sold the rights to tax those needing to travel to brokers. They in turn contracted with fishermen. Fishing families often formed cooperatives to create a better bid for those contracts. It is likely the Zebedee family was in a business partnership with Simon Peter for this very reason.[4]

Soon after Jesus was baptized, he spent an extended period in Capernaum. It was there he called several of his disciples to follow him, including Salome's two sons. It is likely Jesus shared many meals with the family, giving Salome the opportunity to hear his teachings and converse with him at length. Luke tells us that Salome eventually traveled with Jesus as he went from town to town proclaiming the kingdom of God. She was a part of a group of women who financially and physically contributed to the entire entourage.[5]

Who was really making the request?

Matthew seems to indicate that while Salome was the one speaking to Jesus, the request was not hers. First, it is recorded that Jesus did not answer Salome directly; rather, Jesus directed his response toward her sons. Second, when the other disciples responded in indignant anger to the request, they did not direct their anger toward Salome. They were furious with James and John. In Mark's account, he did not mention Salome at all. He recorded the conversation as taking place with James, John, and Jesus.[6]

As outrageous and boldly self-serving as the request might seem, James and John's request is not surprising in view of how they are portrayed in the rest of the Gospels. Jesus nicknamed the men Sons of Thunder, a label fitting men audacious in speech. And that they were: an example is recorded in Luke, when they responded indignantly to a refusal of hospitality by a Samaritan village. "Lord, do You want us to command fire to come down from heaven and consume them?" they angrily asked him.

Jesus was quick to rein in their condemning anger. "You do not know what kind of spirit you are of," he rebuked them. "For the Son of Man did not come to destroy men's lives, but to save them."[7]

In Mark's record, the wording of James and John's request for the most important places of honor is downright shocking: "Teacher, we want You to do for us whatever we ask of You."[8] What would lead them to feel free to make such a demand of the Son of God?

On several occasions Jesus took James, John, and Peter aside for private instruction. They were also the only ones privileged to witness Jesus raising Jairus's daughter from the dead as well as the Transfiguration. Did their status as part of the inner circle of three prompt such boldness with Jesus?

There is also a possibility their request was based on a familial relationship. In later writings, there is speculation that Jesus, James, and John were actually cousins.[9] This assumption most likely comes from a comparison of gospel accounts. Matthew, Mark, and John listed the women present at the crucifixion. Matthew recorded the women as Mary Magdalene; Mary, the mother of James and Joseph; and the mother of Zebedee's sons.[10] Mark named Mary Magdalene; Mary, the mother of James the Less and Joses; and Salome.[11] John's list is slightly different, at least in how he identified the women. He named Mary, the wife of Clopas; Mary Magdalene; Mary, the mother of Jesus; and the sister of Jesus' mother.[12]

Assuming that Mary, the wife of Clopas, in John is the same woman as Mary, the mother of James and Joses (or Joseph), this would make the wife of Zebedee the sister of Jesus' mother. This interpretation, of course, assumes that the three gospel writers are listing the very same three women, which may or may not be the case. But if it were true, that would make the boldness of James and John's request a little more understandable. As extended family, it would not be unreasonable to assume they would play a privileged role in Jesus' kingdom.

What kind of kingdom were Salome and her sons envisioning?

Their request demonstrates their belief that Jesus had

come to establish a powerful earthly kingdom. This conviction reflected the common Jewish messianic expectations of their day.

The Old Testament prophets consistently declared the message that one was coming who would restore Israel to self-rule and glory. He would establish peace and abundantly supply the nation's physical and spiritual needs. The nation eagerly anticipated the coming of that Messiah. They were miserable under the oppressive occupation of Rome. They earnestly desired deliverance from their political and physical bondage.

Yet political victory was only half of what God revealed concerning the Messiah. Right alongside predictions of a deliverer were descriptions of a suffering Messiah, despised and rejected, bearing the sin of the world:

> *He was pierced through for our transgressions,*
> *He was crushed for our iniquities;*
> *The chastening for our well-being fell upon Him,*
> *And by His scourging we are healed.*[13]

The Jewish expectations of Salome's day were based on the one characterization, but ignored the other.

What the Jews did not see was that the Messiah was coming twice. When Jesus came the first time, it was to bear the sin of the world. He accomplished that very thing, conquering sin's hold on us by enduring the wrath of God on the cross and then resurrecting from the dead. Forty days later, as he left the earth, he assured his disciples that this was not the end. He will come a second time—at the end of the age—to rule the earth from Jerusalem and bring peace to Israel, fulfilling the promises made so long ago.[14] That kingdom will be set up at the time of his return, his second coming, sometime in our future. Two comings, with two very different agendas. Salome and the Jews of her day did not understand this. So their expectations of Jesus during his first coming were doomed to be unfulfilled.

What was the cup to which Jesus referred?

There are two nuances of possible meaning about the cup of which Jesus spoke to James and John. First, a cup was a metaphor often used in the Old Testament to describe God's judgment and wrath.[15] This picture was in the forefront of Jesus' mind, as demonstrated in his response to James and John: "The Son of Man did not come to be served, but to serve, and to give His life a ransom for many." Jesus knew his dying would serve a purpose: by suffering the wrath of God in our place, he would make payment for our sin and set us free.[16] He would give his life for ours.

Second, at the time of his arrest, Jesus referred to the ordeal he was about to endure as the cup: "My Father, if it is possible, let this cup pass from Me; yet not as I will, but as You will."[17]

While the cup of suffering under the wrath of God was what Jesus was about to experience, was he telling the disciples they would be required to suffer the wrath of God as well? This does not make sense in light of other teachings of Scripture. The sacrifice Jesus made was a one-time event that paid the necessary price of sin for all people for all time.[18] Only he could make the payment for the sin of others because only he was sinless. How can you pay for someone else's guilt if you yourself are guilty? For these reasons, Jesus could not have meant they would suffer the wrath of God as he would. God's wrath would be forever satisfied by his sacrifice alone.

So what did Jesus mean when he told the disciples they would drink the cup?

In ancient days the king customarily handed the cup to his guests at a royal banquet. The act eventually became known as a metaphor for the life and experience that God handed out to men. Psalm 23:5 uses the metaphor in just this way:

> You prepare a table before me in the
> presence of my enemies;
> You have anointed my head with oil;
> My cup overflows.

During his earthly existence, Christ experienced a great deal of suffering. It was not limited to the hours he hung on the cross, enduring the wrath of God. His hometown rejected him; even his family thought he lost his mind. (His brothers did not believe in him until after the resurrection.)[19] He endured denunciation and cruelty from the religious establishment. As he traveled from place to place, he was denied the most basic comforts. As he told a potential follower: "The foxes have holes and the birds of the air have nests, but the Son of Man has nowhere to lay His head."[20] His disciples frequently misinterpreted his words and failed to emotionally support him in his hour of need. On the night of his arrest, he was beaten beyond recognition and later spat upon by the crowds of Jerusalem as he made his way to Golgotha. Soldiers mocked him and cast lots for his clothing. Jesus' suffering went far beyond the cross.

To follow the suffering Messiah would mean to walk in his footsteps, inevitably experiencing in some way what he experienced. Their commitment to him would eventually cost all of the disciples the ultimate price. Jesus told his disciples at the Last Supper: "I have given you a model to follow, so that as I have done for you, you should also do. . . . No slave is greater than his master nor any messenger greater than the one who sent him."[21] James would be murdered by Herod for his belief, and John was relegated to solitary confinement on the island of Patmos until he died.[22] In suffering for his name's sake, James and John would share the cup of Christ.

Where did the disciples go wrong?

While Jesus consistently focused on God and the importance of a heavenly mind-set, the disciples had trouble absorbing the new perspective. They continued to hear what Jesus taught from an earthly viewpoint. But God's kingdom cannot be understood through that lens.

They wanted a Messiah acknowledged as king by all Israel and even Rome. Ironically a Roman official did crown and dress him in a robe. But it all was done in mockery: his crown was a crown of thorns, and the robe was put on to make him a spectacle as the soldiers beat him beyond recognition. All Israel did look up to him, but not as he sat on a throne: instead it was as he hung on a criminal's cross.

But God's kingdom is like that. As Jesus told them, man's ideas of greatness and God's ideas were polar opposites. It would be an upside-down, backward kind of kingdom, at least according to human ideals. The standard of greatness would not be a wielding of power to one's own gain. The standard of greatness in the kingdom of God would be the cross.

The disciples' request demonstrated their lack of understanding. Immediately preceding their request, Jesus had once again laid out his destiny as he told them: "The Son of Man will be delivered to the chief priests and scribes, and they will condemn Him to death, and will hand Him over to the Gentiles to mock and scourge and crucify Him, and on the third day He will be raised up."[23] Jesus was going to Jerusalem in an attitude of servanthood, not privilege. It is hard to understand how the disciples would even think to make such a request in light of the attitude he was so clearly displaying.

The answer to such shortsightedness is in the disciples' focus. They were all about the here and now, limited by an earthly driven perspective. They needed to widen their horizons. It was time to start thinking with a heavenly mind-set.

Hebrews 11 describes this mind-set. After listing a number of Old Testament saints who pleased God with their faith, the writer offered the perspective necessary for that kind of life: "All these died in faith, without receiving the promises, but having seen them and having welcomed them from a distance, and having confessed that they were strangers and exiles on the earth . . . They desire[d] a better country, that is, a heavenly one. Therefore God is not ashamed to be called their God; for He has prepared a city for them."[24] For the most part, the rewards and privileges of the kingdom of God will not be seen in this world. They are reserved for a time beyond this earth so that we can enjoy them for eternity.

James and John were focused on the immediate future. God had plans to reward their faithful service. They needed to think past the present and direct their gaze toward eternity.

For Today's Woman

The disciples had already been promised positions of authority in the kingdom. In chapter 19, immediately before the events concerning Salome and her sons, Jesus told them: "You also shall sit upon twelve thrones, judging the twelve tribes of Israel."[25] Their dedication to Jesus would be rewarded in the kingdom. But apparently that was not enough for James and John. They wanted more. They wanted privileged roles, places of honor. They wanted to be seated at the right hand and the left hand of Jesus. No chance of hiding behind pretended altruistic motives in this bold request! It was all about them. A large helping of pride motivated their request.

Theirs was not a minor mistake. If allowed to continue uncorrected, it would become a barrier to effective leadership, the very thing for which Jesus was grooming them.

There are two kinds of leaders in this world. One leads by command, sending orders down from on high. There is no sense of comradeship, no sense of basic empathy for those under his dictatorship. This is captured in New Testament writings by the Greek word *arche,* most often translated "ruler, prince, or chief." It indicates a leader who is first in importance and power. The term would apply to those in an absolute, no-objections-dared role. It would have been a familiar word to any first-century New Testament reader.

Yet rather than use the word *arche*, when Scripture instructs leaders, it uses the Greek word *kephale*. This is usually translated "head," characterizing leadership far differently. This kind of leader operates right alongside the troops. He is the first to go into battle and leads by example rather than control. The troops follow him wholeheartedly because he commiserates with them in hardship and treats his position as one of service. This second kind of leadership should characterize leaders in the kingdom of God.

Peter clearly reinforced this idea when he exhorted church elders: "Shepherd the flock of God among you, exercising oversight not under compulsion, but voluntarily, according to the will of God; and not for sordid gain, but with eagerness; nor yet as lording it over those allotted to your charge, but proving to be examples to the flock."[26] Leadership in God's kingdom is all about selfless service.

Misuse of power is commonplace in today's society. Power corrupts. Take a good look at world leaders and you will see the pattern repeated. What is the point of being the ruler if you can't bend the rules to suit your purposes? What leader has not forced others to compromise their standards in order to give him what he seeks? It's the way of the world. But it is not the way of God's kingdom.

Humility is seen by the world as a disadvantage, not a virtue. But humility is not weakness at all. It is a voluntary submission, putting our agenda, power, and abilities under God's authority.

"Blessed are the meek," Jesus taught his disciples, "for they shall inherit the earth."[27] The Greek word, *prays*, translated "meek," was used in those days to describe three different things: medicine, wind, and a colt that had been broken.[28] Each possesses power. Medicine has potential to cure an illness. Wind can move a large vessel from one shore to another. A colt under harness can be used to accomplish much hard labor. But each of these things, when not under control, can cause great damage. Medicine, when taken in extreme amounts, can kill the patient. If you have ever been in the winds of a hurricane, you know the destruction that wind can produce. A runaway horse is a danger to anyone in its path. When under control, each of these three can be very beneficial; but when out of control, they can be deadly.[29]

We, too, have much potential power. One powerful instrument we possess is the tongue. James called the tongue "a small part of the body, and yet it boasts of great things. See how great a forest is set aflame by such a small fire!"[30] Our tongues can be used to build or destroy. We have the ability to destroy with a few well-placed words. Yet when yielded to the Spirit, our words can be used to bring peace to calamity, encouragement to the downtrodden, and hope to the hopeless.

A second kind of power we own is the spiritual gifts that God has given us. He has empowered us to build the church. Our gifts are meant to be used in service, for the good of those we serve. They were not given to benefit us. Used incorrectly, they can cause more damage than good! It all depends on the authority under which one is operating.

I know a pastor of a church in Baltimore who takes the idea of service seriously. He enters the scuzziest bars and hands out his business card to every patron with a warm greeting and a handshake. He tells them, "I'm a local pastor, and I am just here to show the love of God in a practical way." Then he

169

rolls up his sleeves and goes to work, scrubbing the dirty, crud-caked bar lavatories until they shine.

You probably won't be surprised to hear that with a dedicated pastor like that, the church is growing steadily. But the new members are not your typical church-hoppers, moving from congregation to congregation in search of a more fulfilling experience. The newer members are alcoholics, drug addicts, and prostitutes, desperate to hear about the love of God. Word has spread quickly on Baltimore streets about the man not afraid to get his hands dirty in service for his King. They come to find out what drives him.

Jesus told his disciples that their acts of service had a definite purpose: "Let your light shine before men in such a way that they may see your good works, and glorify your Father who is in heaven."[31] In our humility, we best reflect the love of God. The kingdom of God is not about seeking self-fulfillment. It is about showing Christ to others. We do it by imitating the life he led on earth. We show him by our humble service.

A third kind of power we possess is our freedom in Christ. While we once were slaves to sin, we have now been declared innocent, out from under the condemnation that was once ours. Paul wrote, "Sin shall no longer be your master, because you are not under the law, but under grace."[32] Sin no longer has a deadly hold on us. Our salvation has come not by following the rules, but by receiving grace.

If Jesus paid for every one of my sins on the cross, then I will never suffer for them. Does this give me freedom to do what I want, with no fear about my future in heaven? Yes, but to do so would be a gross misuse of freedom. Paul wrote the

Romans, "When you were slaves to sin, you were free from the control of righteousness. What benefit did you reap at that time from the things you are now ashamed of? Those things result in death! But now that you have been set free from sin and have become slaves to God, the benefit you reap leads to holiness, and the result is eternal life."[33] Remaining a slave to sin will put us on a road to destruction. Voluntarily placing our freedom in God's hands and submitting ourselves to him will keep us from destroying ourselves.

"You were called to freedom, brethren; only do not turn your freedom into an opportunity for the flesh, but through love serve one another," Paul wrote the Galatians.[34] Putting the power of our freedom under God's authority will allow us to use it for good rather than cause destruction. Peter concurred: "Act as free men, and do not use your freedom as a covering for evil, but use it as bondslaves of God."[35]

Meekness is not weakness. It is power under control. If we are to serve effectively in the kingdom of God, we must place all of who we are and all of what we possess in submission to God's will and plan. It is not about us. It is about how he chooses to reveal himself to the world through us. We are most effective as conduits when we hand our potential power over to him.

As Salome and her sons learned that day, being someone in the kingdom of God means selfless service, not self-promotion.

Ironically, grasping on to our agenda of gaining prestige or a sense of significance is to travel down a road that leads us away from the very thing we desire. It's said that John Rockefeller, the oil tycoon, was once asked how much money was enough. His answer: just a little bit more. When we seek self-fulfillment, we will never get enough to be satisfied. Material goods, power, or influence will bring only temporary relief. Like a drug addict, we will need more and more to satisfy our need. Satisfaction will remain frustratingly out of our grasp.

True fulfillment can come only in doing things God's way. There is no greater joy than being used by him to help others come to a deeper knowledge of God. There is no greater peace than when you are at the center of his will for you.

Like John, James, and Salome, we need to learn the importance of living lives of service rather than striving for self-importance if we are to be effective in the kingdom of God. It will involve sacrifice, and it will involve suffering. After all, we are following a Savior who freely gave in these ways. It is the way of the kingdom. But in the end, it will be worth it all. God will not forget our willingness to put ourselves aside in the interest of showing him to the world. We just need to keep a heavenly mind-set in order to live out the here and now under the gentle authority of our King.

❧ Food for Thought ❧

1. Some Christians believe God will protect them from anything bad that might come along if they just pray hard enough or have enough faith. How does this sense of entitlement size up with what Scripture teaches about suffering? See 1 Peter 4:12–14 and John 15:18–21. What can we realistically expect from God? Read 2 Corinthians 4:7–10.

2. Read Hebrews 11:13–16 and Philippians 3:14–21. Where should our focus be? What does it mean to have a heavenly mind-set as opposed to an earthly driven perspective? What practical examples of this are possible in your everyday life?

3. Suffering is a tool used by God to transform the lives of those who believe. What positive things come from suffering? See 2 Corinthians 4:16–18; James 1:2–4; and 1 Peter 4:1.

4. How do the world's ideas and definitions of greatness compare with what Jesus taught about greatness in the kingdom of God? How did Jesus demonstrate this with his life? See Philippians 2:5–8.

❧ *Journaling* ❧

There are two styles of leadership in Scripture noted by two different Greek words: that of a *kephale* and that of an *arche*. An *arche* is an autocrat who imposes strict control on those under his authority. His power is not questioned, and the decisions he makes are carefully obeyed. Have you seen this kind of leadership enacted in a church? How effective was this kind of rule?

Scripture teaches leaders they should exhibit a different kind of leadership: that of a *kephale* (see 1 Peter 5:3). This kind of authority leads by example and does not lord it over those under his care. He is in the trenches with the troops, struggling alongside those he is responsible to lead. Have you been fortunate enough to experience this kind of church leadership? How did it affect your response to their authority?

What does this tell you about spiritual leadership and its

connection with servanthood? Write a brief description of what a godly leader should look like. Think of the roles you have in your own life that involve leading others. How should these ideals affect the way you conduct yourself with others?

chapter nine

Now on the first day of the week Mary Magdalene came early to the tomb, while it was still dark, and saw the stone already taken away from the tomb.

So she ran and came to Simon Peter and to the other disciple whom Jesus loved, and said to them, "They have taken away the Lord out of the tomb, and we do not know where they have laid Him."

So Peter and the other disciple went forth, and they were going to the tomb. The two were running together; and the other disciple ran ahead faster than Peter and came to the tomb first; and stooping and looking in, he saw the linen wrappings lying there; but he did not go in. And so Simon Peter also came, following him, and entered the tomb; and he saw the linen wrappings lying there, and the face-cloth which had been on His head, not lying with the linen wrappings, but rolled up in a place by itself. So the other disciple who had first come to the tomb then also entered, and he saw and believed. For as yet they did not understand the Scripture, that He must rise again from the dead. So the disciples went away again to their own homes.

But Mary was standing outside the tomb weeping; and so, as she wept, she stooped and looked into the tomb; and she saw two angels in white sitting, one at the head and one at the feet, where the body of Jesus had been lying. And they said to her, "Woman, why are you weeping?"

She said to them, "Because they have taken away my Lord, and I do not know where they have laid Him." When she had said this, she turned around and saw Jesus standing there, and did not know that it was Jesus.

Jesus said to her, "Woman, why are you weeping? Whom are you seeking?"

Supposing Him to be the gardener, she said to Him, "Sir, if you have carried Him away, tell me where you have laid Him, and I will take Him away."

Jesus said to her, "Mary!"

She turned and said to Him in Hebrew, "Rabboni!" (which means, Teacher).

Jesus said to her, "Stop clinging to Me, for I have not yet ascended to the Father; but go to My brethren and say to them, 'I ascend to My Father and your Father, and My God and your God.'"

Mary Magdalene came, announcing to the disciples, "I have seen the Lord," and that He had said these things to her.

—JOHN 20:1–18

(THIS STORY IS ALSO RECORDED IN MARK 16:9–11.)

Unlikely Witness

JESUS AND MARY MAGDALENE

Jesus lay cold in the grave, and for two days Mary grieved her loss. At first light after the Sabbath, Mary Magdalene goes back to the tomb. She is astonished to find Jesus, living and breathing, risen from the dead. Their short encounter at the grave leaves the reader puzzled. Why did Mary return to the grave in search of the body after the angels had already told her Jesus was risen? Why did Jesus tell Mary to stop clinging to him, when he allowed other women to hold his feet and the disciples to touch his wounds later that evening? And why would Jesus choose to reveal himself to Mary (a woman) first?

She gave up tossing and turning and got out of bed. It had been a second long night. One glance at the window told Mary the sun had not yet begun to make its appearance. How appropriate. The gloom of the night perfectly matched her feeling of despair. Jesus had often spoken of spiritual darkness. She now saw and felt what he meant.

Mary splashed water on her face, steeling herself for the day ahead. She tried to stop reliving the horror of that terrible day but found it impossible to erase the scenes from her mind. Nothing in her life could have prepared her for what she witnessed less than forty-eight hours earlier. Everything she had been living for, everything that lent meaning to her life, had simply evaporated as she watched her beloved Lord bow his head and give up his spirit. How could she go on?

No, she couldn't think beyond today, this morning. There was a final task to be done. One more time she must go to the grave. The burial had been done in haste on Friday, the hour of the Sabbath rapidly approaching. Joseph and Nicodemus barely had time to get Jesus' body to the tomb, let alone adequately prepare him for his final rest. Jewish custom called for a fitting burial. While Roman law denied him a proper funeral procession, she could at least do this for Jesus. Tears rolled down her face as she gathered the spices and prepared to depart for the tomb.

There was a tap on her door. Outside stood James's mother, Mary, Joanna, Salome, and several others. As previously arranged, they had come to accompany Mary to the tomb. She embraced her dear friends, and they wept together once more in grief and despair. They knew the teacher well. They had followed him from his early days in Galilee to his final Passover celebration here in Jerusalem. Each woman had faithfully supported Jesus and his disciples with service and monetary gifts. For many months they had listened in rapt attention to the amazing teachings of Jesus, witnessed his miracles, and watched him train the disciples. He had a way of making each of them feel loved and accepted. No one had ever treated them with the kindness and respect as he had. These months had been the best of their lives.

Now his lifeless, tortured body lay cold in the grave. Their sorrow was too great to bear.

Had it been just a few days earlier that Jesus rode into the city on the colt of a donkey, the crowds waving palm branches and shouting, "Hosanna"? Only earlier last week that he sat on the steps of Solomon's Porch and taught the crowds anxious to hear his wisdom? How had the tables so quickly turned? In a few head-spinning hours, Jesus had been arrested, tried, and found guilty of treason. He had been beaten beyond recognition in the hours preceding his death sentence. Arriving at the scene of the crucifixion, the women stood helplessly by, watching their Lord slowly dying. With every hour that passed, the weight of his body made it increasingly harder to fill his lungs. What suffering he endured! It was a gruesome, cruel death.

When it was over, John gently led Jesus' mother, Mary, away from the scene. The other women remained there, unwilling to leave. Crucified criminals typically hung for days, birds of prey and other wildlife picking at the corpses, left as a warning to all those who passed the horrific scene. Joseph of Arimathea approached the women and asked if the family would be claiming the body. The women shook their heads. Mary was in no position to provide a burial for her son. The disciples were nowhere to be found. Would they just have to walk away and allow the indignity to continue even after his death?

Joseph nodded his head. He was a man of means. Just recently he requisitioned a family tomb to be dug out of the rock in a nearby hillside, which had yet to be used. The body could be interred there. But before they could bring Jesus down from the cross, official authorization must be obtained. Joseph bravely decided to identify himself with Jesus by going to Pilate and requesting permission to bury him.

He returned sometime later with Nicodemus and several servants. They carried a hundred pounds of spices and linen strips to wrap the body. No time was to be wasted. The hour had grown late, and the beginning of the Sabbath was approaching. The men loosed the corpse and carried it away to Joseph's tomb. The women followed silently behind the pitiful procession, aware that outward signs of mourning for a crucified criminal were against the law. Yet they could not tear themselves away from their beloved teacher.

The grave had been hewn out of rock on a nearby hillside that held dozens of similar sites. It was typical of the graves of its caliber: a large opening led to an antechamber, at the back of which was a small rectangular doorway leading to the inner chamber. This six- to seven-foot square room had a stone shelf cut into the rock, which ran parallel with the wall. It was on this shelf that the men laid the body of Christ. They quickly washed him, then wrapped him with the linen strips, sprinkling the spices between layers as they worked. They must cease all labor before the Sabbath arrived.

The women remained outside, weeping. It was not long before the men reappeared at the entrance of the tomb. They turned to seal the grave. A groove ran in front of the opening to guide the circular stone into place. The heavy stone moved downhill as the men, aided by gravity, pushed it into place.

As the small group left the garden, several of the women expressed concern about how thorough a job the men had been able to do in such a short time. They agreed to meet the morning after Sabbath to revisit the grave and reassure themselves all was in proper order.

Now, two days later, as the morning sky began to lighten, the women walked back to the gravesite. One of the women thought of the large stone that had been rolled into place to seal the grave. How on earth would they be able to move that heavy stone, uphill of all things, away from the entrance to the tomb? Discouraged, but still determined, the women continued up the hill. Somehow they would make it happen.

When they reached the garden, they were shocked to see the stone had been rolled away from the entrance. Who would disturb the gravesite? Something was not right. Had the disciples been there? Unlikely, since they weren't around to see to his burial. As far as the women knew, the disciples were afraid to give any public show of support for Jesus for fear for their own safety. Would Pilate have disturbed him? That didn't make much sense. He had seemed to want to distance himself from the whole affair, his unusual permission to bury the body evidence of his reluctance to sentence Jesus in the first place. Grave robbers? Joseph of Arimathea? The women stood, discussing in frightened whispers who might have disturbed the grave. What would they see when they entered the tomb?

Then without warning, two men appeared before them. It was immediately apparent these were no ordinary men. They had come from out of nowhere. Their clothing glowed with a bright light in stark contrast to the early-morning semidarkness. Immediately the women bowed to the ground in fear and trepidation. Clearly they were in the presence of heavenly beings.

"Don't be alarmed," the men assured the frightened women. "You are looking for Jesus the Nazarene, who was crucified. He is not here! For he has been resurrected, just as he said! Come and see the place where he lay." Trembling, the women lifted their heads and slowly rose to their feet. They obediently moved to the entrance of the tomb and peered inside. The body was gone. Shock filled Mary as she tried to comprehend what she was seeing. What could all of this mean?[1]

Then the angels reminded the women, "Remember how he spoke to you when he was still in Galilee, saying, 'The Son of Man must be betrayed into the hands of sinful men, be crucified, and rise on the third day?'"[2] Mary remembered those very words coming from Jesus on several occasions. None of it seemed to make sense at the time—so much of what Jesus taught was hard to understand.

The women looked at each other in terrified amazement. Could it be true? Was he not here because he had been raised from the dead? He had resurrected Lazarus and the widow's son. But he was alive when he performed those miracles. How could he perform a miracle on himself if he was already dead?

The angels confirmed their thoughts with their next words. "Go quickly. Tell his disciples and Peter. He has been raised from the dead. In fact, he is going ahead of you to Galilee; you will see him there."[3]

The women turned from the grave and hurried downhill toward town. Their legs could hardly carry them fast enough. He was alive! The message they carried would change everything for the disciples, who were at this moment hiding in fear and sorrow. They could hardly wait to report what they had seen and heard.

They burst into the building where the disciples had been staying. Out of breath, heart almost beating out of her chest, Mary was the first to get words out: "He's risen! We went to the tomb and it was empty! Two angels appeared to us and said Jesus has been raised from the dead!" The other women began to talk at once, adding details in rapid succession.

Most of the disciples viewed the excited and winded group with skepticism. Most had been awakened by the women's noisy arrival and were still rubbing the sleep from their eyes. What were these women babbling about? Obviously they were hysterical. The strain of the previous two days had put them over the top. Jesus was dead, and what they had invested in during the past three years no longer existed. It was over.

Peter and John jumped to their feet. They wanted to see what the women were going on about for themselves. They started out for the tomb.

Mary left the others and followed the two men at a slower pace, still out of breath from her run from the tomb just minutes before. The disciples' doubtful response had shaken her joy. Was Jesus' body really resurrected? Or had the angel maybe meant his spirit was resurrected? But then why was the body gone? By the time she arrived back at the garden, Peter and John had already come and gone. The stone remained rolled away from the opening of the tomb. What was she to think? Fresh tears began rolling down her face. Finally she decided to take another look.

As she bent over to look into the opening, she was astonished to see the two angels now sitting where Jesus' body had been laid on Friday night. "Woman, why are you crying?" one asked, perplexed that she would return to the empty grave. They had already told her Jesus had risen from the dead. Why was she back and still weeping?

Her reply told the angels why the tears still fell. She had not yet fully understood what had happened here. "Because they have taken away my Lord," she told them, "and I don't know where they've put him."

Perhaps it was the expression on the angels' faces as they looked past her and saw Jesus standing in the doorway. Perhaps it was a noise Jesus made as he stood there. Something made Mary turn around and spot him. He repeated the same question the angels just asked. "Why are you crying, woman?"

Mary did not know who this man was. He questioned her like someone in charge and was there very early in the day, too early to be a visitor. She guessed he was the gardener. "Sir, if you have carried him away, tell me where you have put him, and I will get him," she pleaded.

Jesus said, "Mary!" That one word, that voice, calling her by name as he had so many times before, was suddenly achingly familiar. She turned, dismay and sorrow breaking into hope and incredulous joy. He was alive! Hardly believing her eyes, she rushed to Jesus and threw her arms around him.

"Rabboni!" she cried. This was no figment of her imagination. He was real flesh and bone, raised from the dead, heart beating and lungs breathing. The impossible had happened. Now the tears that streamed down her face were tears of joy. With the strength of the desperation she felt to keep him from somehow slipping away, Mary clasped him close to her heart.

Jesus chuckled at her enthusiastic embrace. He understood

what she felt. "Don't cling to me," he gently reassured her. "I have not yet returned to the Father. Go instead to my brothers and tell them, 'I am returning to my Father and your Father, to my God and your God.'"

She understood. The disciples had scoffed at her previous report. But now she had seen the Lord face-to-face. She had wrapped her arms around his living, breathing body. She had heard his voice and looked him in the eye. The disciples needed to know what she knew and right away. Reluctantly she released Jesus, turned away, and headed down the path, anxious to do his bidding.

Digging Deeper

Who was Mary Magdalene?

We don't know a lot about Mary Magdalene. Scripture gives us only short glimpses of her, but her name is mentioned twelve times. This is unusual for a female in the Gospels—only Mary, the mother of Jesus, is mentioned more often. When identified as part of a group of women, she is named first in the group eight out of nine times. This may be because of her importance as the first witness to the resurrection. It could also be because Mary Magdalene may have been a leader in the early church, and her name would have been immediately recognized by first-century readers.

Mary Magdalene came from the town of Magdala, located in the region of Galilee, the northernmost region of Israel, where Jesus began his ministry. It was located three miles northeast of Tiberias. Sometime early in Jesus' ministry, Luke tells us

Jesus delivered Mary from demons that inhabited her body.[4] Looking at other gospel accounts of demon-possessed people, we can know he rescued her from a miserable existence. All four Gospel writers describe demon-possessed people as having wildly erratic behavior, uncontrollable outbursts, convulsions, and seizures. Sometimes their behavior was so violent, people could not pass by where they lived for fear of coming to harm. Some demons even caused blindness or muteness. Many possessed people lived in the elements among the tombs. It must have been a frightening, painful way of life.

We don't know about Mary Magdalene's specific exorcism other than she was delivered by Jesus. Luke tells us she was inhabited by seven demons. The number seven is often symbolically used to express completeness in Scripture. It could be that Luke's specifically citing seven demons was another way of expressing their complete domination of Mary. She had totally lost control. After she had been transformed from such a tortured existence, her heart must have been overwhelmed with gratitude. Rather than return to her family or hometown, she chose to become a disciple of Jesus, following him from town to town, hearing his teaching, and watching him minister to the sick and needy.

It was not unusual for a teacher like Jesus to have a group of disciples under his tutelage. His group of followers included far more than the twelve we normally associate with Jesus.[5] However, Luke's mention of this group of women, who traveled with the group, providing for Jesus and his followers "out of their own resources," was highly unusual.[6] The fact that Jesus traveled with women would have raised eyebrows at the least, and most likely would have been considered shameless and illicit conduct.[7] Most of the women were probably single, as they apparently had control over their financial resources.[8] Early Jewish literature confirms that well-to-do women often contributed to rabbis and their students.[9] But women actually traveling with a rabbi was certainly not the norm.

Bible scholars through the years have speculated that Mary was a prostitute before becoming a Christ follower. In the sixth century, Pope Gregory the Great interpreted the gospel accounts of Luke's sinful woman, Mary of Bethany, and Mary Magdalene as being the same person identified in different ways.[10] The Catholic Church later rejected this idea.[11] There is no scriptural evidence for any of this. Any information about Mary Magdalene beyond what is clearly indicated in the Gospels is speculation.

Why did Mary report the resurrection news to the disciples, then turn around and go back to the tomb, still looking for a body?

Did Mary not believe the angels' announcement? Or had she believed and then changed her mind?

To attempt conjecture on what Mary was probably thinking, we need to examine first-century Jewish beliefs about resurrection. The idea of resurrection had emerged from several Old Testament prophecies. Isaiah 26:19 promises God will resurrect those who belong to him:

> *Your dead will live;*
> *Their corpses will rise.*
> *You who lie in the dust, awake and shout for joy . . .*
> *[T]he earth will give birth to the departed spirits.*

Ezekiel 37:1–14 records a vision of dry, dead bones being resurrected, bringing a great army to life. Daniel 12 also prophesied a time when those written in "the book" will be brought to life from the dust of the ground. In each case, the idea of bodily resurrection is portrayed not in individual occurrences, but in the resurrection of the nation. When the resurrection occurred, it would happen to all of God's chosen people at once.

Another first-century idea about resurrection concerned the temporary separation of body and soul. This idea was developed in other ancient writings. In Wisdom 3:1, the souls of the righteous are described as being in God's hand. In 1 Enoch 37–70, which many first-century Jews considered Scripture, disembodied spirits are described as alive but waiting for a new bodily life to begin.

What did first-century religious leaders teach about resurrection? While the Sadducees rejected the notion of any possibility of resurrection, the Pharisees fully embraced the idea.[12] It eventually became a political doctrine for them; they believed that God would overcome the present world powers and restore Israel to political freedom and power once more.[13] Some believed he would do this through a Messiah, who would defeat their enemies and set up a kingdom to rule the world.

If Mary had heard these teachings prevalent in the synagogues and temple, she might not have understood the angels' announcement of Jesus' resurrection as we do in hindsight today. Could Jesus have risen from the dead without his body? This could possibly have been how Mary understood the angels' announcement, since she was still concerned about the whereabouts and postmortem care of Jesus' body. Inquiring about the body did not necessarily attest to disbelief in the angels' announcement earlier that morning. Luke tells us that the angel reminded them of Jesus' prediction that he would rise again on the third day, "and they remembered His words."[14] Once they did, they ran from the tomb to carry the good news to the disciples. They certainly seemed to believe something about what the angels said.

If Mary Magdalene surmised that Jesus' resurrection was in spirit only, she might well have assumed his body would remain in the grave until the final resurrection when all Israel would be bodily raised from the dead. Therefore she could have believed the angels, yet still be concerned that the body be properly prepared for interment.

Why was it so important to Mary that the body be properly prepared?

The Jews believed that providing a proper burial was a serious responsibility for those left behind.

Usually a funeral was a weeklong affair. After death, the body was washed, then wrapped in strips of cloth interspersed with more than one hundred pounds of expensive spices. Relatives and close friends ripped their clothing and sprinkled ashes on their heads as an outward expression of their grief.[15] Friends and family gathered around the corpse, wailing and lamenting.[16] Professional mourners were often hired to attend the events.[17] A funeral procession then moved through the streets from the place of death to where the body was to be interred.[18] As the mourners marched through the streets, anyone who happened to be nearby was compelled to join their ranks.[19]

The followers of Jesus were not to have the opportunity to honor Jesus in any of these ways. Crucifixion was a punishment for high treason against the Roman Empire, and there were strict limitations on what could be done for a crucified criminal after his death. A public funeral procession was absolutely prohibited for a crucified criminal—in fact, every type of public mourning was illegal. The Romans' normal procedure was to leave a body on the cross for days, to eventually be torn to shreds by predatory wild animals and birds.[20] This was considered a part of the horror of crucifixion and meant to be a deterrent to would-be criminals. The practice was extremely offensive to the Jews, who believed an improper disposal of a body actually cursed the land. After all, the Law prescribed the immediate burial of someone who died by hanging before sundown.[21]

Jesus died at 3:00 p.m., the very hour the sacrificial lamb was offered for Passover. This left just a few hours to get him down from the cross, adequately prepare him for interment, and finally place him in a tomb before darkness fell, signaling the onset of the Sabbath. No family member came forth to request the body, but Joseph of Arimathea did. Joseph was a member of the Sanhedrin,[22] the religious council that condemned and brought Jesus before the Roman authorities to be sentenced to death. By claiming the body, Joseph was taking a huge risk: it declared sympathy and association with a condemned criminal, and the authorities could look suspiciously at his action.

Yet he went. He and Nicodemus, another Pharisee, returned with the materials necessary to prepare the body, probably with servants to aid in the urgent, time-sensitive task. Joseph and Nicodemus did everything technically correct,[23] but the haste with which they had to do it probably bothered Mary Magdalene and the other women. He couldn't have a proper funeral, but they could give him a proper burial. Thus at first daylight, the women returned after the Sabbath to satisfy their sense of propriety.

Jesus had been dead more than thirty-six hours. It would not be a pleasant task to tend to a body that had already begun to rapidly decompose in the heat of the climate. A Jew would have especially abhorred the task, since a corpse was categorized as unclean by the Law. Those who attended to the body would be considered unclean for seven days following their labor.[24] Mary Magdalene and her friends must have been intensely devoted to be willing to even approach the tomb at that point.

Why didn't Mary recognize Jesus right away?

Mary was not alone in her inability to recognize Jesus. Jesus joined two disciples on the road to Emmaus for the seven-mile journey. They carried on a long conversation with him as they walked, but did not realize they were speaking with Jesus. It wasn't until they sat down to break bread together that their eyes were opened and they finally recognized him.

The scriptural accounts of the post-resurrection appearances of Jesus indicate his resurrected body was different from his pre-crucifixion body. Jesus could appear and disappear, moving through a closed door to visit with his disciples. But he did have a physical resurrected body because the disciples felt his wounds. Jesus urged them to do so to correct their assumption that he was only "a spirit." Mary Magdalene clung to him, and the other women "took hold of" his feet.[25] He also ate in the disciples' presence on more than one occasion.

The people whom Jesus raised from the dead did not have this kind of body, however. Lazarus came out of the grave still wrapped in his grave clothes, "bound hand and foot with wrappings, and his face was wrapped around with a cloth."[26] Jesus had to tell the mourners to unbind him and let him go.[27] Yet the resurrected Jesus seemingly passed right through his grave clothes; they were left lying on the shelf.[28] Another difference was the resurrected Lazarus could not go through obstacles as Jesus did. Before Jesus raised Lazarus from the dead, he instructed that the stone be removed from the tomb entrance. This was presumably so that Lazarus could get out. (Lazarus would experience a second death eventually; Jesus would not, but ascend to heaven. Perhaps this might explain the difference.)

In view of the obvious differences in the pre- and post-resurrected Jesus shown in these instances, perhaps his appearance was altered enough to have made recognition difficult. Or perhaps God caused the inability to recognize him. When the disciples on the road to Emmaus were approached by Jesus, Luke tells us "their eyes were prevented from recognizing Him." Later in the day as they broke bread with Jesus, Luke wrote, "Then their eyes were opened and they recognized Him."[29] Their ability to recognize him and understand he was their resurrected Lord came from God, much like our ability to understand all spiritual matters.[30]

Why did Jesus tell Mary to stop clinging to him?

This is an intriguing question, for Jesus let the other women take hold of his feet and the disciples touch his wounds. Why then did he tell only Mary to stop touching him?

I can imagine the moment Mary realized she was with Jesus in the flesh. When my mother died, I used to imagine that she would walk through my door, whole and well, as if the tragedy of her death was just a bad dream. How thankful I would be to be able to speak with her again! There was so much I hadn't said, so much gratitude I hadn't expressed while she was still living. If I could just have one hour with her, I would be so grateful.

Mary had been grieving for two days. She thought that she would never see or speak to Jesus again. Imagine the joy that welled up from her heart when she realized he was back. Any decorum she might have observed in the past, any limitations of expression necessitated by acceptable social appropriateness, would have been flung to the side as she rushed to embrace the one she loved with all of her heart. Would he disappear as quickly as he had appeared? She probably couldn't hold him tight enough to appease her intense desire to keep him with her. The Greek verb Jesus used to describe her action, *haptomai,* is best translated in this context as "clinging."

I can imagine Christ's delight in her spontaneous response. He may have even laughed a little in pure joy as he spoke to her. "Stop clinging to me! I have not yet ascended to the Father." In other words, Jesus was telling Mary: Don't worry. I'm not going anywhere just yet. You don't need to cling to me. I'll be around for some time before I go back to heaven.[31] (He would not ascend to the Father for forty days, as recorded in Acts 1.)

Why was Mary Magdalene, of all the disciples, chosen to see our resurrected Lord first?

It is a little puzzling that Mary would have been the one chosen to first witness the resurrected Lord. Why not Peter, John, or James, the three in Jesus' innermost circle? Why a woman? Jewish law at the time did not even consider the testimony of a woman valid in a court of law.[32] Yet women were given not only the first news of his resurrection, but Mary was the first to see the resurrected body of Christ.

Don't think for a moment it was by accident that Mary was first to see the Lord. Nothing about the crucifixion or resurrection happened by chance. Each event was carefully orchestrated by a sovereign God, fulfilling the prophecies given long ago. The plans had been in place before the foundation of the world.

Certainly the disciples did not believe the women's story. Luke said their words appeared to the disciples as "nonsense," and they refused to believe what they said.[33] So you can imagine how the rest of the Jewish community would respond to their witness! So why did God choose a woman?

The fact that Jesus even had women accompanying him in his travels shows a definite disregard for what was acceptable conduct according to first-century Jewish culture. Women were second-class citizens in those days. In each interaction with women, Jesus lifted and liberated them to equality with men unprecedented in their society.

At the fall, God decreed a consequence for each participant

in the original sin. One consequence for Eve was a change in her relationship with her husband. He would now rule over her.[34] Before the fall, Adam and Eve had an equal partnership, man and woman valued equally with equivalent responsibilities. With the onset of sin, this all changed.

Jesus came to conquer sin and its consequences and accomplished this when he rose from the dead. No longer would a woman be treated as a less valuable entity than a man. "There is neither Jew nor Gentile, neither slave nor free, nor is there male and female, for you are all one in Christ Jesus," Paul assured his readers.[35] In the kingdom of God, women have been redeemed from the consequences of sin, brought back to their original standing before the fall. In Christ they have been set free.

Perhaps God was demonstrating this fact to the world when he gave Mary Magdalene the great privilege of being the first to witness the resurrected Lord.

Another possible answer is in seeing how God delights in choosing opposite to the world's standards to demonstrate his glory. Paul expressed this thought in his letter to the Corinthians: "God has chosen the foolish things of the world to shame the wise, and God has chosen the weak things of the world to shame the things which are strong . . . so that no man may boast before God."[36] As mentioned earlier, a woman was not considered to be a valid witness. She was thought unworthy to be taught the truths of the Talmud or to sit under the tutelage of a rabbi.[37] To the first-century world, choosing a woman made no sense at all. But it makes perfect sense in the context of how God tends to operate.

Why specifically Mary Magdalene? Mary had a story to tell. While utterly helpless, she had been rescued from complete demonic domination to become a beloved disciple of the Son of God. Now she had been given the extraordinary privilege of being the first to see the resurrected Jesus in the flesh. Who was Mary Magdalene to be given such a position? The answer: no one. And that was what God wanted. He wouldn't choose the self-made man or woman. He wants the glory and deservedly so. He wants the world to understand that it is all about him—his work, his grace, his glory.

God expressed that same idea to the Jews in Deuteronomy as they prepared to enter the promised land. He wanted them to understand that their status as God's people had nothing to do with their merit: "The LORD did not set His love on you nor choose you because you were more in number than any of the peoples, for you were the fewest of all peoples."[38] God chose to reveal his strength through their weakness. Then there would be no doubt he was the source of power.

Mary was in a perfect position to give God the glory. He extended grace and mercy to her when the demons were exorcised from her body. He restored her, gave her a reason to live and a place in his household. She overflowed with gratitude for what he did in her life. She couldn't bear to be apart from him—even in his death.

As mentioned earlier in chapter 3, Jesus once asked the Pharisee Simon, "A moneylender had two debtors: one owed five hundred denarii, and the other fifty. When they were unable to repay, he graciously forgave them both. So which of them will love him more?"

Simon answered, "I suppose the one whom he forgave more."

And Jesus said to him, "You have judged correctly."[39]

Those who have been given much will love much. Mary was an excellent candidate to share her deliverance and consequent experience with the world. God had plans to use her story to bring glory to his name.

For Today's Woman

Who are you? "No one," you might be tempted to answer. That may be true to the rest of the world, but not in God's eyes. He has redeemed you from a condemned status. He has taken your brokenness and fixed what ailed you. He has loved you completely, through no merit of your own. He has lavished you with grace and supplied every need. You, like Mary Magdalene, have been given much. God has plans to use your story to bring glory to his name as well.

Feelings of inadequacy can paralyze us, preventing us from doing the work of God. Before every retreat at which I speak, I look in the mirror and wonder why anyone would bother to listen to this overweight middle-aged woman. In our culture, appearance is everything. Countless shows on TV chronicle makeovers where women go from frumpy to fantastic. They emerge at the end of the show, confident in their new hair, makeup, and wardrobe, twirling and showing off their new look to family and friends. I am a makeover wannabe.

Yet the truth of the matter is this: when it comes to sharing truth about Christ, neither smooth talking nor a beautiful appearance is where the power lies. I was amused and rather struck to find this in Paul's second letter to the Corinthians about himself: "For they say, 'His letters are weighty and strong, but his personal presence is unimpressive and his speech contemptible.'"[40] Paul wrote strong letters, filled with astounding truth and depth. Yet when those who had heard his written words actually met him in person, they were shocked. Who was this dumpy, inarticulate guy? Could he actually be the author of such profound writing?

Our effectiveness has never been about us at all. We are mere messengers. The power is in the message. God's Word is powerful and effective. It changes lives. The Lord promised Isaiah:

> *For as the rain and the snow come down from heaven,*
> *And do not return there without watering the earth*
> *And making it bear and sprout . . .*
> *So will my word be which goes forth from My mouth;*
> *It will not return to me empty,*
> *Without accomplishing what I desire,*
> *And without succeeding in the matter for which I sent it.*[41]

God will use his Word to accomplish his purposes. Success in its mission is not limited to our expertise in presenting it at all. The power and effectiveness lie in the truth of the message. Paul's writing was a result of the work of the Holy Spirit. The power in its words was the power of God, not the power of Paul.

Mary was given a message to share. The Lord had risen. He conquered the power of death and defeated sin's hold on us forever. By his resurrection he proved himself to be the Son of God. Mary's job was to simply relate what she knew through personal experience to anyone who would listen.

It wasn't about Mary at all. It was about the Lord revealing himself through her. And so it is with us. We need to focus on the Message Maker, not the messengers that we are. And God will be faithful to reveal himself to the world through our obedience.

❧ Food for Thought ❧

1. Read Romans 8:1–4; 15–17. Then read John 8:36. Jesus set us free from the condemnation of sin and its ensuing consequences. How can a woman serving in today's church reflect this truth?

2. Read 2 Corinthians 1:3–5. Mary Magdalene had a unique experience with the Lord. Yet the experience was not to benefit Mary alone. She was given the command (twice!) to "go and tell." How has Christ affected your life? What experience have you been given to pass on that might benefit others?

3. What is your biggest weakness? How does it impact your confidence about bearing testimony about the Lord? Read 2 Corinthians 4:6–7 and 12:7–10. What is promised here? How can your inadequacy be a conduit through which God reveals his glory?

4. Before she was born, God had decided that Mary Magdalene would be the first witness to the resurrection (see Ps. 139:16). Ephesians 2:10 tells us God has prepared good works for us as well. To what specific good works has God called you? Read Ephesians 4:16. What can you personally contribute to the building up of the church?

5. Read Isaiah 55:10–11. How does this promise give you confidence in passing on God's message?

❧ *Journaling* ❧

How does Mary Magdalene's story influence how you think about your place in the kingdom of God? How practically will this affect your life this week?

Conclusion

——

$\mathcal{N}$ ine women.

Nine cryptic conversations.

Nine encounters with the Savior, whose carefully spoken words changed everything.

As I concluded my study on these incredible conversations, I began to wonder: Why these nine women? Was there some common thread that made them notable enough to include in the Gospels?

It seems that our first-century sisters came from all walks of life. Several appear to have come from money; others were financially destitute. Some lived in good standing within their community. Others were regarded as sinners and unclean. Most were Jews; but two of the women had gentile blood. In other words, about the only thing these women shared as a group was that they had little in common.

But one exception unifies the whole lot. Every one of them needed Jesus Christ.

Were they conscious of their need? Almost certainly

the Samaritan woman had other things on her mind as she approached the well in the midday sun. The adulterous woman sprawled on the temple courtyard was likely more concerned about a possible death sentence than her spiritual condition. Some approached him to solve a merely physical problem, unaware of their more pressing issue. Yet some, like the sinful woman, were well aware of their sin and craved the grace he offered.

But aware or not, every one of them needed Jesus in her life. Yes, they needed him to fix their immediate presenting problem. But in reality they needed so much more. They needed forgiveness and mercy. They needed peace with God. They needed hope.

Jesus came to bring these things and more.

One more thing becomes obvious as we read of his interactions with these women: he was *interested*. Each one he encountered, whether humble or proud, seeking or oblivious, had his complete attention. He was intentional in his conversations with them. He used his knowledge of them to coax them into a relationship with him. No matter what their initial intentions might have been, as he spoke with them, there was no one more important on this earth.

My friend directs the band program at a large Christian school where I used to teach. For many years, part of her job was to produce an annual variety show that enjoyed schoolwide student participation. For several years I assisted her in managing the enormous group of students on stage. One thing that never ceased to amaze me was her personal interest in each student, no matter how young, how insignificant their part, how silly the question might be, or how many students waited in line behind them to speak with her after a rehearsal. Each child had her complete attention as he or she spoke. Every one was equally important. For this (and many other reasons), the students unequivocally loved their director.

We all have a need for significance, a need to feel that we matter. In my faith, at times I have struggled to believe I could be significant to God. After all, he is busy running the universe, for goodness' sake. Far more important people are praying for his help and direction. Why in the world should I think he would be interested in someone as insignificant as me?

Having the opportunity to watch Jesus in these accounts reveals the fallacy of that thinking. He *is* interested. His concern does not depend on how spiritual I might be or how important I might seem in human eyes. It is not dependent on my performance or even my good intentions. I matter to him not because of who I am or what I do. I matter because of who he is.

"Jesus Christ is the same yesterday and today and forever."[1] He is still the same Savior today as he was to the first-century women of the Gospels. He can calm a powerful storm with a word, yet weeps with us when we weep. He can heal the sick and raise the dead, yet makes it his business to involve himself in the small, seemingly insignificant details of our lives.

He is interested. If you take nothing else away from this book, tuck this truth in close to your heart. He will never fail to meet you where you are when you come to him. All he asks in return is for your trust. And even then, faith as small as a mustard seed is enough. He is crazy about you.

Acknowledgments

---

*B*ack in 2004, God planted a dream in my heart. I would write a book.

The fulfillment of a dream is rarely accomplished alone. There are so many people who allowed God to use them in encouraging me down the long road to publication. I cannot hope to name you all, but I would like to thank everyone who has given me a kind word or feedback in my teaching and writing efforts. The body of Christ needs each other: it's how God set up his church to function. This has been demonstrated to me in a very practical way as I have endeavored to take this journey.

The faculty at Capital Bible Seminary was instrumental in giving me the skills to dig deep, enabling me to tap into the richness of God's Word. In particular, I'd like to thank Ken Quick, who taught me to always reach for the chocolate macadamia cookies on the top shelf; Jonathan Master, who lit a fire under me to develop the kind of theology that would serve as a firm foundation to whatever I studied; and James Davis, who taught me Greek (no easy task, that one!) and excellence in biblical research.

Thank you, Davey Ermold, for your constant willingness to research the Greek when questions arose.

For those who offered practical support along the way, I thank you: especially Linda Coleman, who voted with her checkbook, financially supporting my attendance at many writers' conferences over the years. I am so grateful to author Kathi Macias, whose kind interest in this fledgling writer led to my acquiring an agent and ultimately a contract. I also thank my agent, Steve Hutson, for his guidance in developing the right angle for my proposal and for landing me the opportunity of a lifetime.

My family has been a constant source of support and encouragement. I am a mother truly blessed to be so well loved. Thank you, Adam and Ruth, Daniel and Bethany, Joe and Liz, and Melanie, for your interest, constant support, and willingness to read my work. Your belief in my chasing this dream has meant the world to me.

I leave the most important thank-you for last. Words cannot express the gratitude I have for my husband, Steve. You have selflessly supported me from the very beginning. I'll never forget the first time I allowed you to read my work. You were so enthusiastic and immediately saw its potential. You encouraged me to leave my teaching career behind and go to seminary, ready to trust God for the financial challenges that decision would present for our family. You believed in the dream more strongly than I ever could, and your unflinching support carried me through times of doubt and discouragement. We both know the book could not have been written without your wisdom, spiritual insight, excellent revision input, and practical support. I love you with all my heart, Steve. Thank you for making my dream your own. You have demonstrated with your life what true oneness is all about.

Notes

Introduction

1. Philo wrote that man's attitude was informed by reason, while a woman's mind was ruled by her sensuality. Joan E. Taylor, "Spiritual Mothers: Philo on the Women Therapeutae," *JSP* 23 (2002): 41–43.

2. "It was taught: Do not speak excessively with a woman lest this ultimately lead you to adultery." *b*Ned.201.

3. William Barclay, *The Gospel of John*, vol. 1 (Louisville, KY: Westminster John Knox Press, 2001), 176.

4. Aristotle once wrote, "We should look upon the female state of being as though it were a deformity, though one which occurs in the ordinary course of nature." Aristotle, *Metaphysics*, quoted in Rosalind Miles, *The Women's History of the World* (Topsfield, MA: Salem House, 1989), 57.

5. A woman could not travel without permission from her husband. She did not receive an education. She was expected to remain at home to raise children and was banned from taking part in much of public life.

6. BT *Sotah* 21b; *j*Sota, 10a, 8.

7. Traditional prayer.

8. Genesis 2:22–25.

9. Genesis 3:16.

10. 1 Corinthians 6:20.

Chapter 1: Mother Doesn't Always Know Best

1. Howard F. Vos, *Nelson's New Illustrated Bible Manners and Customs* (Nashville, TN: Thomas Nelson Publishers, 1999), 449.

2. Ronald F. Youngblood, gen. ed., *Nelson's New Illustrated Bible Dictionary* (Nashville, TN: Thomas Nelson Publishers, 1995), 580–81.

3. Luke 1:31–35.

4. Matthew 1:21.

5. Luke 1:43.

6. Luke 2:11.

7. Luke 2:25–38.

8. Matthew 2:11.

9. Luke 2:19.

10. Matthew 2:13–14.

11. Matthew 2:19–23.

12. Luke 2:51.

13. Lisa Sergio, *Jesus and Woman* (McLean, VA: EPM Publications, 1975), 11.

14. It is generally assumed that Jesus' father, Joseph, died sometime between Jesus' ages of twelve and thirty, since the temple

incident was the last time he appeared in the Gospels. Many believe that was why Jesus waited until age thirty to begin his earthly ministry: he was caring for his mother and family after Joseph's death until the next relative was ready to take on the responsibility.

15. Luke 2:52.
16. Mark 1:10–11.
17. John 1:51.
18. William Barclay, *The Gospel of John,* vol. 1 (Louisville, KY: Westminster John Knox Press, 2001), 115.
19. John 19:26–27.
20. Luke 8:28, see also Matthew 8:29; Mark 1:24; Luke 4:34.
21. Exodus 20:12.
22. Matthew 15:3–6.
23. John 7:4, 8, emphasis added.
24. John 7:10, emphasis added.
25. John 7:30; 8:20.
26. John 12:23–27.
27. John 1:31–33.
28. John 4:14.
29. Barclay, *The Gospel of John,* 1:115.
30. Youngblood, *Nelson's New Illustrated Bible Dictionary,* 7.
31. Mark 2:22.
32. Amos 9:13.
33. Luke 1:38.
34. Luke 1:46–55.

35. Job 42:1–6.

36. Psalm 139; Matthew 10:30.

37. Psalm 56:8.

Chapter 2: Embarrassed or Expunged?

1. Leviticus 15:33.

2. Talmud cures. See J. Preuss, *op.cit.*, pp. 439f.; S-BK I (1922), 520. Cited in William L. Lane, *The Gospel According to Mark,* NICNT (Grand Rapids, MI: Eerdmans, 1974), 192n.

3. Leviticus 5:3.

4. Leviticus 15:21.

5. Deuteronomy 24:1 NKJV.

6. Leviticus 15:29–31.

7. Lane, *Gospel According to Mark,* 192. As part of the purifying process, Leviticus 15:27 and 17:15 prescribe washing the clothing of a person who has become unclean.

8. Matthew 14:36. Since this occurred sometime after the healing of the hemorrhaging woman, the request may well have originated from the news of her healing.

9. In Acts 19:11–12 we read that "God was performing extraordinary miracles by the hands of Paul, so that handkerchiefs or aprons were even carried from his body to the sick, and the diseases left them and the evil spirits went out."

10. Isaiah 55:8.

11. Joel B. Green, *The Gospel of Luke,* NICNT (Grand Rapids, MI: Eerdmans, 1997), 349.

12. Luke 8:50.

13. Matthew 9:22.

14. Mark 5:36.

15. William Barclay, *The Gospel of Mark* (Louisville, KY: Westminster John Knox Press, 1975), 126.

16. Ephesians 1:4–5.

17. Merrill C. Tenney, gen. ed., *Zondervan Pictorial Bible Dictionary* (Grand Rapids, MI: Zondervan, 1967), 15.

18. Galatians 4:7.

19. 1 Peter 1:18–19.

20. Ephesians 1:13, 19–20.

21. Ephesians 3:20.

22. Hebrews 4:15–16; Romans 2:4.

23. Philippians 4:7, 19.

24. Philippians 1:6.

25. Hebrews 12:5–11.

26. Matthew 28:20; Romans 8:38–39.

Chapter 3: Grateful Extravagance

1. Merrill C. Tenney, gen. ed., *Zondervan Pictorial Bible Dictionary* (Grand Rapids, MI: Zondervan, 1967), 647–48.

2. Ibid.

3. Ibid.

4. Matthew 15:2.

5. Mark 2:23–28.

6. Romans 9:31–32.

7. Matthew 6:2, 5, 16.

8. Matthew 23:3.

9. Bauer-Danker-Arndt-Gingrich. *A Greek-English Lexicon of the*

New Testament and Other Early Christian Literature. 3rd ed., (Chicago: University of Chicago Press, 2000), 1038.

10. Matthew 5:20.

11. John 19:38–40.

12. Acts 9:1–19.

13. Joel B. Green, *The Gospel of Luke,* NICNT (Grand Rapids, MI: Eerdmans, 1997), 310.

14. William Barclay, *The Gospel of Luke* (Louisville, KY: Westminster John Knox Press, 1975), 95.

15. Barbara Reid, *Choosing the Better Part?* (Collegeville, MN: Liturgical Press, 1996), 116.

16. John 9:2.

17. Jeffrey John Kripal, *The Serpent's Gift: Gnostic Reflections on the Study of Religion* (Chicago: University of Chicago Press, 2007), 52.

18. In 1969 the Vatican rejected this teaching and separated the identities of Luke's sinful woman, Mary of Bethany, and Mary Magdalene.

19. Numbers 27:8.

20. Reid, *Choosing the Better Part?,* 121.

21. Acts 18:2–3.

22. In Luke 5:17–26, friends brought a paralytic to Jesus to be healed. Jesus told him, "Friend, your sins are forgiven you." The scribes present at the healing had a severe reaction and asked, "Why does this man speak this way? He is blaspheming; who can forgive sins but God alone?" In the Old Testament, God alone had the authority to forgive sins. In their eyes, Jesus'

assuming of that kind of authority was to disrespect the majesty and authority of God.

23. Green, *Gospel of Luke*, 314.

24. Romans 5:17, 20; Ephesians 1:6–7; 2:7–8.

25. Romans 5:20.

26. Romans 5:18.

27. Mark 2:17.

Chapter 4: Adding Insult to Injury?

1. "The demon has gone out of your daughter": perfect tense. Indicative of a perfect cure. Kenneth S. Wuest, *Wuest's Word Studies from the Greek New Testament*, vol. 1 (Grand Rapids, MI: Eerdmans, 1973), 153.

2. Krister Stendahl as quoted in William L. Lane, *The Gospel According to Mark*, NICNT (Grand Rapids, MI: Eerdmans, 1974), 6.

3. W. F. Albright, *Yahweh and the Gods of Canaan* (Garden City, NY: Doubleday, 1968).

4. Francis Taylor Gench, *Back to the Well* (Louisville, KY: Westminster John Knox Press, 2004), 19.

5. William Barclay, *The Gospel of Mark* (Louisville, KY: Westminster John Knox Press, 1975), 178.

6. Ibid.

7. Helen Bruch Pearson, *Do What You Have the Power to Do* (Nashville, TN: Upper Room Books, 1992), 82.

8. James 2:9–10.

9. Hebrews 4:15.

10. Matthew 1:3, 5.

11. John 10:14–16, emphasis added.

12. Matthew 15:11; Mark 7:15.

13. Matthew 15:18–20.

14. Paul confirmed this concept in his letter to the Ephesians 2:14–16: "He Himself is our peace, who made both groups into one and broke down the barrier of the dividing wall, by abolishing in His flesh the enmity, which is the Law of commandments contained in ordinances, so that in Himself He might make the two into one new man, thus establishing peace, and might reconcile them both in one body to God through the cross, by it having put to death the enmity." Peter had the same lesson reiterated for him in Acts 10:9–23.

15. Remember the Lord's Prayer: "Give us this day our daily bread" (Matt. 6:11). See also Arthur B. Fowler, "Bread," in *The Zondervan Pictorial Bible Dictionary*, ed. Merrill C. Tenney (Grand Rapids, MI: Zondervan, 1967), 132.

16. Gench, *Back to the Well*, 12.

17. 2 Corinthians 12:9.

18. John 15:6.

19. Revelation 3:17.

20. Revelation 3:18.

Chapter 5: Fork in the Road

1. Leon Morris, *The Gospel According to John*, NICNT (Grand Rapids, MI: Eerdmans, 1995), 779.

2. Zane Hodges makes an argument for Johannine authorship in his article "The Woman Taken in Adultery (John 7:53–8:11):

The Text," *Bibliotheca Sacra* 136 (October-December 1979):
318–32.

3. Mark 3:6. The Herodians were normally a group vehemently
opposed by the Pharisees. Contrary to popular first-century
Jewish sentiment, they had pro-Roman sympathies and supported Greek customs and Roman law. The very fact the
Pharisees were willing to partner with them in this common cause demonstrates the amount of hatred the Pharisees
had toward Jesus. They would go to any lengths to see him
destroyed—even associate with the enemy.

4. Mark 12:13–17.

5. Mark 12:17.

6. Ronald F. Youngblood, gen. ed., *Nelson's New Illustrated Bible
Dictionary* (Nashville, TN: Thomas Nelson Publishers, 1995),
1128.

7. Deuteronomy 22:22.

8. Morris, *Gospel According to John*, 782.

9. D. A. Carson, *The Gospel According to John*, PNTC (Grand
Rapids, MI: Eerdmans, 1991), 592.

10. Francis Taylor Gench, *Back to the Well* (Louisville, KY:
Westminster John Knox Press, 2004), 140.

11. Morris, *Gospel According to John*, 783.

12. 2 Peter 3:9.

13. Deuteronomy 17:7.

14. Deuteronomy 19:18–19.

15. See the book of Susanna in the New Revised Standard Version
with the Apocrypha. Note that it is chapter 13 of the Greek version of Daniel.

16. 2 Corinthians 5:17 UPDATED NIV.

17. Ephesians 2:1–3.

18. Romans 8:5–7.

19. 1 Corinthians 2:14.

20. John 3:19; Romans 1:21.

21. 1 Corinthians 2:12; 1 John 5:20.

22. Romans 5:5.

23. Romans 6:14–18.

24. 2 Peter 1:3.

25. The apostle Paul bemoaned the struggle that exists between the spirit and the flesh: "For what I am doing, I do not understand; for I am not practicing what I would like to do, but I am doing the very thing I hate . . . [T]he willing is present in me, but the doing of the good is not . . . Wretched man that I am! Who will set me free from the body of this death?" (Rom. 7:15, 18, 24). That reality is why we continually need grace in order to live a life yielded to the spirit of God who dwells within us. The writer of Hebrews urged us: "Let us draw near with confidence to the throne of grace, so that we may receive mercy and find grace to help in time of need" (Heb. 4:16). Grace saved us, and grace will empower us in our quest to live for him.

26. 2 Corinthians 3:18.

27. Philippians 1:6.

28. Exodus 33:17, emphasis added.

29. Psalm 139:17–18 NLT.

30. Luke 12:7.

31. Psalm 139:2–4.

32. John 21:15.

33. Philippians 3:13–14.

34. Matthew 11:28, 30, emphasis added.

Chapter 6: Misery Wants Company

1. Leviticus 19:34.

2. Job 31:32.

3. Isaiah 58:7, 9.

4. Psalm 23:5.

5. Martha's question begins with the negative particle *ou*, indicating anticipation of an affirmative answer. Here is a suggested paraphrase that reflects this meaning: "Lord, I know you care that my sister has left me to do all the serving alone. Since you do, tell her to help me!"

6. Mark 9:35.

7. Matthew 20:28.

8. Luke 8:21; 11:28.

9. Luke 12:22, 30.

10. Francis Taylor Gench, *Back to the Well* (Louisville, KY: Westminster John Knox Press, 2004), 62.

11. Luke 19:1–6.

12. Luke 10:17.

13. Luke 10:20.

14. Leviticus 19:18.

15. Luke 10:25–28.

16. Luke 10:29.

17. Luke 10:30–37.

18. See Luke 10:30, 38 in the New King James Version.

19. Luke 1.

20. Luke 7:36–50.

21. Luke 21:1–4.

22. 1 Corinthians 13:1.

23. John 11–12.

24. Matthew 16:16.

25. John 20:31.

Chapter 7: Thirsty for More than Water

1. D. A. Carson, *The Gospel According to John,* PNTC (Grand Rapids, MI: Eerdmans, 1991), 216.

2. Mishnah *Niddah* 4:1, cited in Carson, *Gospel According to John*, 217–18.

3. Leon Morris, *The Gospel According to John,* NICNT (Grand Rapids, MI: Eerdmans, 1995), 226.

4. Ronald F. Youngblood, gen. ed., *Nelson's New Illustrated Bible Dictionary* (Nashville, TN: Thomas Nelson Publishers, 1995), 489.

5. Genesis 22:2–4 names the site of Moses' command to erect an altar at Mount Moriah.

6. Deuteronomy 27:4 records the site as Mount Ebal.

7. Joshua 8:30–35.

8. William Barclay, *The Gospel of John,* vol. 1 (Louisville, KY: Westminster John Knox Press, 2001), 175.

9. John 1:33.

10. John 7:38.

11. John 7:39.

12. Lynn H. Cohick, *Women in the World of the Earliest Christians* (Grand Rapids, MI: Baker Academic, 2009), 123.

13. Ibid.

14. Deuteronomy 24:1.

15. Cohick, *Women in the World of the Earliest Christians,* 125.

16. John 3:17 UPDATED NIV.

17. Deuteronomy 18:18.

18. John 14:6 UPDATED NIV.

19. Exodus 3:14.

20. John 18:5–6.

21. In Acts 1:8, the apostles are commissioned to preach to the surrounding Gentiles.

22. Genesis 16:1–15 NIV.

23. Exodus 3:2–4:17; Numbers 22:22–35; Judges 6:11–24.

24. Genesis 16:13; Hagar is the only human recorded in the Bible to have given God a name. Carolyn Custis James, *Lost Women of the Bible: Finding Strength and Significance through their Stories,* (Grand Rapids, MI: Zondervan, 2005), 95.

Chapter 8: Misguided Mother

1. Flavius Josephus, *The Genuine Works of Flavius Josephus,* trans. William Whiston (Boston, MA: W. Borradaile, 1824), 223n.

2. William Barclay, *The Gospel of Mark* (Louisville, KY: Westminster John Knox Press, 1975), 27.

3. Mark 1:19–20; Ronald F. Youngblood, gen. ed., *Nelson's New Illustrated Bible Dictionary* (Nashville, TN: Thomas Nelson Publishers, 1995), 457.

4. Luke 5:10.

5. Luke 8:1–3.

6. Mark 10:35–40.

7. Luke 9:51–56.

8. Mark 10:35.

9. This was first stated by Origen, *In Matthaeum: Commentariorum Series 141,* and later in *Chronikon* by Hippolytus of Thebes.

10. Matthew 27:56.

11. Mark 15:40.

12. John 19:25.

13. Isaiah 53:5.

14. You can read more on this second coming in passages like Isaiah 9:6–7; 11:1–16; 42:1–13; Ezekiel 36.

15. Psalm 75:8; Isaiah 51:17; Jeremiah 25:15–16.

16. John 8:34–36.

17. Matthew 26:39.

18. Hebrews 10:11–14.

19. John 7:5; Acts 1:14.

20. Matthew 8:20.

21. John 13:15–16 NAB.

22. Acts 12:1–2; Revelation 1:9.

23. Matthew 20:18–19.

24. Hebrews 11:13, 16.

25. Matthew 19:28.

26. 1 Peter 5:2–3.

27. Matthew 5:5 NKJV.

28. Warren Wiersbe, *Live Like a King* (Chicago, IL: Moody Press, 1976), 64–65.

29. Ibid.

30. James 3:5.

31. Matthew 5:16.

32. Romans 6:14 NIV.

33. Romans 6:20–22 NIV.

34. Galatians 5:13.

35. 1 Peter 2:16.

Chapter 9: Unlikely Witness

1. Matthew 28:5–6, author's paraphrase.

2. Luke 24:6–8, author's paraphrase.

3. Mark 16:7, author's paraphrase.

4. Luke 8:2.

5. Acts 1:21.

6. Joel B. Green, *The Gospel of Luke,* NICNT (Grand Rapids, MI: Eerdmans, 1997), 318.

7. Ibid.

8. David C. Sim, "The Women Followers of Jesus: The Implications of Luke 8:1–3," *Heythrop Journal* 30 (January 1989): 54–55.

9. Green, *Gospel of Luke,* 185.

10. Jeffrey John Kripal, *The Serpent's Gift: Gnostic Reflections on the Study of Religion* (Chicago: University of Chicago Press, 2007), 52.

11. Mary Alice Williams, "Mary Magdalene," in *Religion and Ethics,* a PBS series, 21 November 2003, episode 712, http://www.pbs.org/wnet/religionandethics/week712/feature.html.

12. The Pharisees and Sadducees were two distinct political factions within Israel's first-century religious leadership. The Pharisees regarded the written and oral law as equally authoritative and insisted on strict adherence to the rules. These men were of the craftsmen class and enjoyed popular support from the people. They believed in the resurrection of the dead. The Sadducees, on the other hand, were aristocrats and priests. They rejected the Oral Law and accepted only the Pentateuch (the first five books of the Old Testament) as authoritative Scripture. This privileged class enjoyed status in society and got along well with Roman authorities. They did not believe there would be a bodily resurrection; they also denied the immortality of the soul (as neither idea is included in the Pentateuch).

13. N. T. Wright, "Jesus' Resurrection: The First-Century Jewish Understanding of Resurrection," 3–4 St. John in the Wilderness Adult Education and Formation, http://www.stjohnadulted.org /resurr3.htm#The%20Scriptural%20Basis%20for%20the%20 First%20Century%20Jewish%20Belief%20in%20Resurrection,.

14. Luke 24:8.

15. Joshua 7:6; 2 Samuel 1:2.

16. John B. Graybill, "Mourning," in *Zondervan Pictorial Bible Dictionary*, ed. Merrill C. Tenney (Grand Rapids, MI: Zondervan, 1967), 561.

17. Jeremiah 9:17–18.

18. Luke 7:12.

19. Christine M. Carpenter, *All the Women in the Bible: The Women Around Jesus* (Portland, OR: CMC Press, 1996), 115.

20. William L. Lane, *The Gospel According to Mark,* NICNT (Grand Rapids, MI: Eerdmans, 1974), 578.

21. Deuteronomy 21:23.

22. Leon Morris, *The Gospel According to John,* NICNT (Grand Rapids, MI: Eerdmans, 1995), 728.

23. John 19:40.

24. Numbers 19:11–13.

25. Matthew 28:8–9.

26. John 11:44.

27. Ibid.

28. John 20:6.

29. Luke 24:16, 31.

30. John 16:13–15; 1 Corinthians 2:14.

31. Morris, *The Gospel According to John,* 728.

32. Lane, *The Gospel According to Mark,* 589. M. Rosh Ha-Shanah 1.8 speaks of the disqualification of women as witnesses as common knowledge.

33. Luke 24:11.

34. Genesis 3:16.

35. Galatians 3:28 NIV.

36. 1 Corinthians 1:27, 29.

37. The subject of women studying the Torah is first addressed in the *Midrash Halakha*: "And you shall teach your sons and not your daughters." The Mishnah (*Sotah* 3:4) expresses opposition to the idea of a woman studying the Torah: "Anyone who teaches his daughter Torah teaches her *tiflut*" (BT *Sotah* 21b).

The word *tiflut* can be interpreted as sexual license or lewdness because knowledge might enable the woman to be smarter than her husband and therefore outwit him by sinning in secret. The *Jerusalem Talmud* states: "The words of the Torah should be burned rather than entrusted to women" (*JT Sotah* 3:4, 19a).

38. Deuteronomy 7:7.

39. Luke 7:41–43.

40. 2 Corinthians 10:10.

41. Isaiah 55:10–11.

Conclusion

1. Hebrews 13:8.

Bibliography

Albright, W. F. *Yahweh and the Gods of Canaan*. Garden City, NY: Doubleday, 1968.

Barclay, William. *The Gospel of John*. Vol. 1. Louisville, KY: Westminster John Knox Press, 2001.

———. *The Gospel of Luke*. Louisville, KY: Westminster John Knox Press, 1975.

———. *The Gospel of Mark*. Louisville, KY: Westminster John Knox Press, 1975.

———. *The Gospel of Matthew*. Louisville, KY: Westminster John Knox Press, 1975.

Bauer-Danker-Arndt-Gingrich. *A Greek-English Lexicon of the New Testament and Other Early Christian Literature*. 3rd ed., Chicago: University of Chicago Press, 2000.

Carpenter, Christine M. *All the Women in the Bible: The Women Around Jesus*. Portland, OR: CMC Press, 1996.

Carson, D. A. *The Gospel According to John*. Pillar New Testament Commentaries. Grand Rapids, MI: Eerdmans, 1991.

Cohick, Lynn H. *Women in the World of the Earliest Christians*. Grand Rapids, MI: Baker Academic, 2009.

Gench, Francis Taylor. *Back to the Well*. Louisville, KY: Westminster John Knox Press, 2004.

Green, Joel B. *The Gospel of Luke.* New International Commentary on the New Testament. Grand Rapids, MI: Eerdmans, 1997.

Hodges, Zane. "The Woman Taken in Adultery (John 7:58–8:11): The Text." *Bibliotheca Sacra* 136 (October-December 1979): 318–32.

James, Carolyn Custis. *Lost Women of the Bible: Finding Strength and Significance through their Stories.* Grand Rapids, MI: Zondervan, 2005.

Jerusalem Talmud. JT Sotah 3:4.

Josephus, Flavius. *The Genuine Works of Flavius Josephus.* Trans. William Whiston. Boston, MA: W. Borradaile, 1824.

Kittel, Gerhard, ed. *Theological Dictionary of the New Testament.* Vol 1. Trans. Geoffrey W. Bromiley. Grand Rapids, MI: Eerdmans, 1964.

Kripal, Jeffrey John. *The Serpent's Gift: Gnostic Reflections on the Study of Religion.* Chicago, IL: University of Chicago Press, 2007.

Lane, William L. *The Gospel According to Mark.* New International Commentary on the New Testament. Grand Rapids, MI: Eerdmans, 1974.

Midrash Halakha.

Morris, Leon. *The Gospel According to John.* New International Commentary on the New Testament. Grand Rapids, MI: Eerdmans, 1995.

———. *The Gospel According to Matthew.* Pillar New Testament Commentary. Grand Rapids, MI: Eerdmans, 1992.

Pearson, Helen Brunch. *Do What You Have the Power to Do.* Nashville, TN: Upper Room Books, 1992.

Reid, Barbara E. *Choosing the Better Part? Women in the Gospel of Luke.* Collegeville, MN: The Liturgical Press, 1996.

Sergio, Lisa. *Jesus and Woman.* McLean, VA: EPM Publications, 1975.

Sim, David C. "The Women Followers of Jesus: The Implications of Luke 8:1–3." *Heythrop Journal* 30 (January 1989): 54–55.

Taylor, Joan E. "Spiritual Mothers: Philo on the Women Therapeutae." *Journal for the Study of the Pseudepigrapha,* 23 (2002): 37–63.

Tenney, Merrill C., gen. ed. *Zondervan Pictorial Bible Dictionary.* Grand Rapids, MI: Zondervan, 1967.

Vos, Howard F. *Nelson's New Illustrated Bible Manners and Customs.* Nashville, TN: Thomas Nelson Publishers, 1999.

Wiersbe, Warren W. *Live Like a King.* Chicago, IL: Moody Press, 1976.

Williams, Mary Alice. "Mary Magdalene." *Religion and Ethics,* a PBS series. 21 November 2003. Episode 712. http://www.pbs.org/wnet/religionandethics /week712/feature.html.

Wright, N. T. "Jesus' Resurrection: The First-Century Jewish Understanding of Resurrection." St. John in the Wilderness Adult Education and Formation. http://www.stjohnadulted.org/resurr3.htm#The%20 Scriptural%20Basis%20for %20the%20First%20Century%20 Jewish%20Belief%20in%20Resurrection.

Wuest, Kenneth S. *Wuest's Word Studies from the Greek New Testament.* Vol. 1. Grand Rapids, MI: Eerdmans, 1973.

Youngblood, Ronald F., gen. ed. *Nelson's New Illustrated Bible Dictionary.* Nashville, TN: Thomas Nelson Publishers, 1995.

About the Author

*J*ulie Coleman is dedicated to helping others understand the Bible's
message and experience its transforming
power. After twenty years of teaching
young minds, she turned in her chalk
and left the classroom behind to earn
an MA in biblical studies from Capital
Bible Seminary. In addition to full-time

PHOTO COURTESY OF ANGIE RICH

writing and speaking, Julie and her husband, Steve, like to
spend as much time as possible with their four children, their
spouses, and six grandchildren. They make their home in the
Annapolis, Maryland, area.

You can learn more about Julie and her ministry at
www.juliecoleman.org. Be sure to sign up for her free bi-weekly
e-mail newsletter, *The Dogwood Digest*!

Free resources, including handouts and lesson plan sug-
gestions, are available for groups using *Unexpected Love* at
www.unexpectedlove.org.